I0374630

بسم الله الرحمن الرحيم

SPIRITUAL DISCOURSES

SPIRITUAL DISCOURSES

Murtaḍā Muṭahharī

Translated by

Alauddin Pazargadi

Edited by

Salman Tawhidi

British Library Cataloguing-in-Publication Data
A catalogue record for this book is available from the British Library.

ISBN: 978-1-907905-10-0 (hbk)
ISBN: 978-1-907905-11-7 (pbk)

This English edition first published in 2013

MIU Press
133, High Road, Willesden
London NW10 2SW

Contents

Transliteration ... *IX*
Publisher's Note ... *XI*
Biography of the Author ... 1
Discourse 1: The Criteria for Humanity ... 5
Perfected and Unperfected Man ... 5
1. Attitude ... 6
2. Philanthropy ... 7
3. Will ... 9
4. Freedom ... 9
5. Responsibility and Burden ... 11
6. Beauty ... 11
Discourse 2: The School of Humanity ... 13
Fall of Humanity in Recent Centuries ... 13
Reappearance of Humanity and the Occurred Contradiction ... 15
Absolute Peace ... 16
The Fundamental Difference between Man and Animals ... 17
The Religion of Humanity "Auguste Comte" ... 18
Man's Freedom and Responsibility ... 19
Man's Happiness and Pleasure ... 20
Contradiction in the School of Humanism ... 21
The Relation between Humanism and God ... 24
Discourse 3: Spiritual Freedom I ... 27
The Term *Mawlā* ... 27
The Meaning of Freedom and Liberty ... 29

Kinds of Freedom 30
Social Freedom in the Qur'an 31
Spiritual Freedom 33
Dependence of Social Freedom upon Spiritual Freedom 34
The True Liberal Man 36
Discourse 4: Spiritual Freedom II 41
Man: A Complex Existent 42
Slavery of the Spirit 42
Slavery with regard to the Wealth 44
Human Ego and Animal Ego 46
Man Judging Himself 47
The Conscience Blames 49
Man Punishes Himself 50
Spiritual Freedom, Prophets' Greatest Plan 51
Discourse 5: Nobility and Magnanimity of Spirit 53
Great Ambition in the way of Knowledge 53
Great Ambition of Gaining Wealth 54
Being Overambitious 55
Graciousness 57
The Holy Prophet's Words 57
Imām 'Alī's Words 58
Damages of Ṣūfīs' Teachings 60
Imām Ḥusain's Words 61
Discourse 6: Worship and Prayer I 63
An Example of Excessiveness in performing Acts of Worship 64
Excessiveness in the consideration of Social Problems 65
'Alī (A.S.) The Perfect Example of Islam 67
Portrait of a Muslim Community 69
Heedlessness of the Prayers 70
Imām 'Alī's Ablution 71
Heedlessness of Other Acts of Worship 73
Discourse 7: Worship and Prayer II 75
Faith as the Supporter of Morality and Justice 75
The Meaning of Innocence 78

The Prayers Being in Company with Other Affairs: 80
1. Social Rights and Purity 80
2. Knowledge of *Qibla* 80
3. Punctuality 81
4. Emotion Controlling 81
5. Gravity 81
6. Peace-Making with all Virtuous People 82
The Influence of the Phrase "God Is the Greatest" 83
Our Responsibility of Encouraging Our Families to Perform Prayers 84
Imām Ḥusain's Prayers in Karbala Desert 85
Discourse 8: Repentance I 87
Analysis of Repentance from a Psychological Viewpoint 88
Man, a Complex Person 89
Conditions of Appearance of Repentance 91
Remembering the Late Ḥāj Mīrzā 'Alī Āqā Shīrāzī 93
Imām 'Alī's Advice 95
A Sacred Tradition 97
The Repentant Of Karbala Desert 98
Discourse 9: Repentance II 101
Opportunity for Repentance 101
Repentance from Imām 'Alī's Viewpoint 104
The First Pillar of Repentance: Regret 106
The First Pillar of Repentance: Decisive Resolution not to Return 106
The First Condition of Repentance: Returning What Belongs to Others 106
The Second Condition: Restoring Heavenly Rights 107
The First Condition of Perfection of Repentance 108
The Second Condition of Perfection of Repentance 108
Two Qur'anic Points 108
A Peculiarity of Prophets and Saints 109
Bishr Ḥāfī's Repentance 110
Abū Lubāba's Repentance 111

Zuhayr Ibn al-Qayn's Repentance 112
Discourse 10: Migration and *Jihād* I 115
Migrating Sins 115
Fighting against Carnal Soul 117
Wrong Interpretation 119
Decisive Intention of Migration and *Jihād* 120
A Dream of a Great Scholar 122
Discourse 11: Migration and *Jihād* II 127
Islam Praises Travelling 127
Superiority of Travelers 129
Migrating Habits 130
Struggling and Removing Obstacles 131
Discourse 12: Belief in the Unseen 135
The Meaning of Unseen 136
The Way of Believing in the Unseen 137
Assistance from the Unseen Is Not Groundless 138
A Story from Āyatullāh Burūjirdī 139
Intellectual's Pessimism about Future of the World 140
Bright Future from a Religious Perspective 140
Bibliography *143*
Index *145*

Transliteration

Symbol	Transliteration	Symbol	Transliteration
ء	’	أ	a
ب	b	ت	t
ث	th	ج	j
ح	ḥ	خ	kh
د	d	ذ	dh
ر	r	ز	z
س	s	ش	sh
ص	ṣ	ض	ḍ
ط	ṭ	ظ	ẓ
ع	‘	غ	gh
ف	f	ق	q
ک	k	ل	l
م	m	ن	n
ه	h	و	w
ی	y	ة	ah
Long Vowels		Short Vowels	
آ	a	ـَ	a
ای	ī	ـِ	i
او	ū	ـُ	u
Persian Letters			
Symbol	**Transliteration**	**Symbol**	**Transliteration**
پ	p	چ	ch
ژ	zh	گ	g

At the end of Farsi words, 'eh', '-e', and '-ye' have been used.

Publisher's Note

Spiritual Discourses is a translation of the Persian book *Guftār-hā-ye Ma'nawī* by the great Muslim thinker and reformer Āyatullāh Murtaḍā Muṭahharī. This book is a collection of thirteen lectures delivered by the Āyatullāh on such various topics as the criteria for humanity, the school of humanity, spiritual freedom, nobility and magnanimity of spirit, worship and prayer, repentance, migration and *Jihād,* and belief in the unseen. As all of these lectures are on spiritual issues, they are gathered in one collection.

The English translation of this book was published many years ago by Muslim Students Association of Europe. Now, Al-Mustafa International Research Institute (M.I.R.I) has the honor to present this book to the dear readers in a new form. In the present edition the biography of the author, transliteration of expressions as well as Farsi and Arabic names, bibliography, index, and some subtitles are added. In addition, existing mistakes are corrected and incomplete references are completed.

We hope that this book will be a valuable contribution to Islamic thought that is of value to the general reader and the researcher alike.

Al-Mustafa International Research Institute (M.I.R.I.)

Biography of the Author

Murtaḍā Muṭahharī was born in a village some forty kilometres from Mashhad in 1338/1919–20. He received his earliest education mostly at the hands of his father and while still a child entered the Ḥawza 'Ilmiyya, the traditional educational establishment, of Mashhad, but soon afterwards left for Qum, the centre for religious education in Iran. While he was pursuing elementary studies there he was greatly affected by the lessons in *akhlāq* (Islamic ethics) given by Āyatullāh Imām Khumaynī, which Muṭahharī himself described as being, in reality, lessons in *ma'ārif wa sayr-u-sulūk* (the theoretical and practical approaches to mysticism). He later studied metaphysics (*falsafa*) with him, as well as jurisprudence (*uṣūl al-fiqh*). He was especially attracted by *falsafa*, theoretical mysticism (*'irfān*) and theology (*Kalām*), known as 'intellectual knowledge', and he went on to study these subjects with 'Allāma Ṭabāṭabā'ī. His teachers in law (*fiqh*) were all important figures of the time, especially Āyatullāh Burūjirdī, who became the authoritative jurisconsult (*marja'-e taqlīd*), as well as head of the ḥawza 'ilmiyya of Qum, in 1945. Murtaḍā Muṭahharī studied both *fiqh* and *uṣūl* al-*fiqh* in the classes of Āyatullāh Burūjirdī for ten years. He was also deeply affected at about this time by lessons on *Nahj al-Balāghah* given by Mīrzā 'Alī Āqā Shīrāzī Iṣfahānī, whom he had met in Isfahan. He later said that, although he had been reading this work since his childhood, he now felt that he had discovered a 'new world'. Subsequently, Muṭahharī became a well-known teacher in Qum, first in Arabic language and literature, and later in logic (*Manṭiq*), *uṣūl al-fiqh*, *falsafa* and mysticism.

In 1952 Murtaḍā Muṭahharī moved to Tehran, where, two years later, he began teaching in the Theology Faculty of the University. Not only did he make a strong impression on students, but his move to Tehran also meant that he could become involved with organizations for political and social change. These Islamic associations were groups of students, engineers, doctors, merchants, etc., set up during the 1950s and 1960s; they formed the nucleus of the movement that was eventually to become the revolution. He was also a founder member of the Ḥusainiyya Irshād, which played a central role in the religious life of the capital during the four years of its existence until its closure by the authorities in 1973. At the same time he maintained his contact with traditional religious activities, teaching first in the Madrasa Marwī in Tehran and later back in Qum, and also preaching in mosques in Tehran and elsewhere in the country. Through his lectures, articles and books he became a famous and much-respected figure throughout Iran, but it was mainly among the students and teachers of the schools and universities that he was most influential, setting an example and inspiring them as a committed and socially aware Muslim with a traditional education who could make an intellectually appropriate and exciting response to modern secularizing tendencies.

His wide-ranging knowledge and scholarship are reflected in the scope of his writings, which cover the fields of law, philosophy, theology, history and literature. He was also one of the few high-ranking *'ulamā* to be in continuous contact with

Imām Khumaynī during the fifteen or so years in which the movement that led to the revolution was developing. He was actively engaged in all the stages of this movement. His life came to an abrupt and untimely end when he was shot in the street by an assassin after a meeting of the Revolutionary Council on the evening of 1 May 1979. Many mourners accompanied his funeral cortege from Tehran to Qum, where he was buried near the shrine of the sister of the eighth Shīʿī Imām. Shahīd Muṭahharī contributed a great deal to Islamic scholarship through his many publications, most of which have been translated into English. They include: Islamic Modest Dress (Macmillan Publishing Company, Inc., 1990); Universal Prototype, translated by Laleh Bakhtiar (Abjad Book Designers & Builders, 1989); Hijab, translated by Laleh Bakhtiar (Abjad Book Designers & Builders, 1993); Iqbal (Abjad Book Designers & Builders, 1993); Reviving Islamic Ethos; Master and Mastership; Jurisprudence and Its Principles; Spiritual Discourses; The Awaited Saviour; Light within Me; The Goal of Life; Man and Universe; Polarization Around the Character of ʿAlī ibn Abī Ṭālib; Woman and Her Rights; and Anecdotes of Pious Men.

Apart from the above-mentioned books, there are many other published works in Arabic and Persian.

Discourse 1
The Criteria for Humanity

I have been asked to discuss the question of the criteria for humanity. If we were to do so from the viewpoint of biology, this would be an easy matter since we would be dealing with the human body and the place of human beings in the animal world, in which case there is no difference between individuals. By the standard of anatomy, medicine, and, even to some extent, psychology, there are no major differences between two or more individuals.

Perfected and Unperfected Man

But is humanity limited to the body? Is human perfection and mobility confined to man's physical aspect? In humanistic sciences there is talk of perfect and imperfect man, of the low and high kind. What type of human being is ethically and socially worthy of respect because of his or her perfection, or deserving of contempt because of his or her imperfections? This is a topic which has always attracted attention not only in human knowledge, but also in various religions. For example, the Qur'an speaks of human beings who are higher than angels and worthy of homage by the latter. It also mentions human beings who are inferior to animals.

What is the criteria which measures the differences between

human beings? This question is not only related to religion. Materialistic philosophers, too, who do not believe in God and religion, discuss the question of man, humanity and superior and inferior beings.

What is the criteria according to these philosophers? Can we say that human beings are equal genetically, but that they differ in knowledge. That is, something which is acquired not inherited, so that a person with more knowledge is higher than one with less? Is this related to academic knowledge which gives superiority according to the level and stage of one's studies? Do we respect people only in proportion to their learning? Is Abū Dharr honoured because he was more learned than his contemporaries? Is Mu'āwiyah blameworthy and disliked because he had inferior knowledge?

I do not believe that learning is a criterion for humanity. If it were so, we should say that Einstein was the most endowed with qualities of humanity since he was the most learned man of his time.

1. Attitude

Another view is that although knowledge is one of the requisites of humanity, and although the importance of awareness of the self, of the society and of the world cannot be denied, it is inadequate. This view claims that humanity is measured by character and disposition. A person may be very learned, but if he has a bad character, would he be considered to be a real human being?

An animal behaves according to its instincts and it possesses no will to rule over its instincts. When we call a dog a faithful animal, its faithfulness is instinctive. An ant is prudent by instinct. There are also human beings in the world who have a disposition resembling that of an animal. They possess their natural instincts, but have done nothing to refine themselves, and are condemned only to follow their nature.

The awareness of an animal is limited to its own time and place, while man's awareness allows him to know the past and have an idea of the future and also step beyond his own area and even his own planet. But the question of character is a different matter. Knowledge is related to what one is taught, while character is related to training and the forming of habits.

I do not think that knowledge as a criterion of humanity is acceptable and I will later explain what type of people support it. The second view, i.e., characteristics as a criterion of humanity, has more supporters. But we may ask what kind of characteristics and dispositions?

2. Philanthropy

One of the answers to this question is that love is the desired criterion, love, which is the mother of other fine dispositions. Thus, if one bases one's character on the love of human beings, one has real humanity. Such a person is as interested in others as in one's self or even more interested in them.

In religion this is called self-sacrifice. There is a statement in a book that there is an instruction in all religions to love for others what you love for yourself, and dislike for them what you dislike for yourself. This has been stated in our traditions.[1] This is the logic of love. As we know, in the Hindu schools and in Christianity, much emphasis is laid on love. But they have gone so far as to lose sight of everything else and maintain that love is to be a course of action in all circumstances. Thus the

1. Imām ʻAlī, *Nahj al-Balāghah*, 397.

love of both these ideologies is a kind of stupefaction and the adequacy of love as a criterion of humanity is to be discussed.

But if we accept the love for other human beings as the criterion, the issue will be solved more easily than if we accept knowledge as the criterion. For example, concerning our preference for Abū Dharr over Mu'āwiyah, we are in a better position to judge them on the basis of love. Mu'āwiyah was a selfish and ambitious man who exploited others by force. Abū Dharr was the reverse, and although he had all the possibilities and even though Mu'āwiyah was prepared to offer him many privileges, yet he was anxious about the fate of others, particularly those who were oppressed by Mu'āwiyah. That is why he arose against this wicked man and spent his last years in exile where he died. Thus, we call Abū Dharr human as he loved others, and we consider Mu'āwiyah inhuman as he was only interested in himself.

Or, similarly, why do we think Imām 'Alī (A.S.), is a perfect human being? Because he felt society's pain, and his 'I' had become 'We'. His personality attracted all others. He was not an individual separated from others. He was a limb or organ of a whole body. He himself said that a pain in one part of society, as in a body, made itself felt in the other parts, one of which was himself. 'Alī had declared this long before the humanistic philosophy of the twentieth century claimed it as an ideal.

When he heard that a governor appointed by him had attended a feast, he wrote him a letter of protest which is quoted in the *Nahj al-Balāghah* . It is not mentioned what kind of a feast it had been, whether there had been drinking or gambling or dancing. The governor was considered guilty by Imām 'Alī (A.S.) because he had participated in an aristocratic feast which was not attended by any poor people.

He says, "I never believed a governor and representative of

mine would attend such a party of the nobility."[1] He then describes his own life and says that he felt other people's pain more than his own and their pain prevented him from feeling his own. His words show that he was a truly learned and wise sage. Yet the reason why we honor him so deeply is not only because of his wide knowledge, but because he was human. He was not unaware of the destiny of others.

3. Will

Another school of thought considers resolution and will power as the criterion for humanity. It claims that if a person can dominate himself, his instincts, nerves and passions by his will-power and reason and not be dominated over by his inclinations and desires, he is really human.

There is a difference between desire and will. Desire is an attraction by an exterior force, a relation between man and external objects, like a hungry man drawn by food, or sexual attraction. Even sleep is an attraction. So is desire for rank and position. But resolution is something internal, which liberates one from the urges of desire. It places desires at the disposal of will-power to employ them as it considers expedient. Most of our past moralists emphasized resolution as a criterion for humanity. People, unlike animals, which are ruled by instinct, can decide to act against their own inclinations. Thus a person of resolution is more human than one who cannot control the 'self'.

4. Freedom

Another criterion for humanity is freedom. What does this mean? It means that to the extent that one tolerates no force, and is not captivated by any power and can choose freely, one is human. In modern schools of thought, much emphasis is laid

1. Ibid, 417.

on freedom as one of the criteria of humanity. Is this view correct or not? It is both correct and incorrect. As a requisite for humanity, it is correct, but as the sole criterion for humanity, it is wrong.

Islam has laid great emphasis on self-control. I relate a story here in connection with it. It is narrated that the Prophet (S) was passing by a place in Medina where a number of young men were testing their strength by lifting a heavy stone. When they saw the Prophet, they asked him to act as judge. The Prophet (S)agreed, and at the end of the competition he said, *"Do you know who is the strongest? It is he who controls his anger and does not allow it to overcome him. He must not use his anger in a way contrary to God's satisfaction and should be able to dominate over his own desires."*[1]

On that day, the Prophet (S) transformed a physical contest into a spiritual one. What he meant was that physical strength shows manliness but it is not the only sign of it. True manliness is in the strength of will power.

We call Imām 'Alī (A.S.) the 'Lion of God', for he was more manly than all in two ways: Externally in society and on the battlefield where he could overthrow his strongest opponents; and, more important than that, internally, meaning that he was in perfect control of himself and of every whim and wish.

Jalāl al-Dīn Rūmī tells a story in his *Mathnawī* about Imām 'Alī (A.S.) as a young man of 24 or 25 in which he portrays a fine picture of manliness. He had thrown down his adversary in a battle and was sitting on his chest, about to kill him. The man spit

1. Muḥammad Ibn al-Ḥasan al-Ḥurr al-'Āmilī, *Wasā'il al-Shī'ah ilā Taḥṣīl Masā'il al-Sharī'ah*, vol. 15, 361.

on Imām's face. Annoyed, Imām 'Alī (A.S.) temporarily leaves the man and walks about for a while. The man asks why he left him to himself. Imām answers, "If I had killed you then, it would have been in anger, not in the way of my duty to my goal and for the sake of God." This is a wonderful example of self-control.

Imām says in his testament to his son, Imām Ḥasan (A.S.), "Consider yourself and your life above every mean deed. In return for what you pay out of your life for desires, you receive nothing. Do not make yourself a slave of others, for God has created you free." [1] The question of freedom is something that the school of existentialism, too, accepts as a criterion for humanity.

5. Responsibility and Burden

Another criterion for humanity is the question of duty and responsibility which began with Kant and has been emphasized in our own time. This means feeling responsible to society, to oneself and to one's family. How should one obtain this feeling and what is its basis? Is it created in one's conscience?

6. Beauty

Another school of thought, including Plato, considers beauty as the criterion for humanity. All schools recognize and approve of justice. One school approves of justice from an ethical viewpoint. Another one approves of it because it considers that there is a relation between justice and freedom, while Plato thinks justice is good in both the individual and society, because it leads to poise and beauty. Of course, his idea of beauty is obviously spiritual beauty.

On another occasion we will judge between all these schools and we will review the views of Islam on this issue.

---

1. Imām 'Alī, *Nahj al-Balāghah*, 401.

Discourse 2
The School of Humanity

The subject of our discourse is 'the school of humanity'. The human being who is the only inquisitive being in the world that we know, has always been subjected to investigation and discussion.

The word 'humanity' has always been connected with a sense of loftiness and sanctity as a being superior to animals from various points of view, such as knowledge justice, freedom, moral conscience, etc. Although many of humanity's sacred objects have been subjected to doubt and even denial, apparently no school of thought has yet gone so far as to scorn the special dignity of humanity and its superiority over other Creatures.

This fact has been elegantly expressed in the poems of Rūmī and Sa'dī and by other poets of ours. This topic is also the theme of most of the world's literature, both religious and non-religious, in which the question of humanity and its glorification has been described. In Islamic literature, too, both in Persian and Arabic, we come across many such statements.

Fall of Humanity in Recent Centuries

In the last two centuries, with the great advance of science, humanity has suddenly fallen from that pedestal of sanctity it had always been given. It fell with a real crash since the more one is elevated, the greater is the damage Caused by the fall. In the past, mankind has been exacted to the rank of a demi-god as witnessed in the poems of Ḥāfiẓ and other poets.

The first discovery of humanity was the form of the universe which revolutionized its ideas. Before that, the earth was believed to be the center of the universe round which all the plants and stars revolved. Science proved that the earth was a small planet which revolved around the sun and the solar System was only an insignificant part of the universe.

It was then that the position of humanity as the center of all possibilities and as the goal of creation was subjected to doubt and denial, and no one dared any longer to make claims about its exalted position. Then, another severe blow dealt, was the idea that the human being was no longer a divine creature and vice gerent of God upon the earth was given up.

Biological research on the question of evolution and the origin of species at once showed the relationship of people with those same animals which they Scorned and despised. It proved them to be an evolved form of a monkey or some other animal and thus they lost their divine origin. Another strong blow as against humanity's apparently brilliant record of activities, namely, that it could act in such a way that showed only goodness and benevolence, whose motive was only the love of Cod, and lacking all animal aspects. The new thesis was that the claim of humanity to all that sanctity and virtue was false and all the activities to which it had given the name of the love of knowledge, art, beauty, morality and conscience, prayer and devotion and everything supernatural, are similar to those which can be found in animals, too, except in a more complex form and mechanism. It was said that the stomach is the source and cause of all activities. Some went so far as to say that the stomach was also the basis of its thoughts and feelings. There were still others who considered this position too high and claimed that the human being was even lower than he is.

Eventually it was concluded that this being who had formerly claimed divine origin and exaltation must be subjected to a careful study to discover its true nature. Another theory was offered that there is no difference between humans, plants and even inanimate objects. There is, of course, a difference in the texture and form, but not in the substance of which they were all made. It was stated that spirit and divine breath were non-existent because the human being is a machine which is only more complicated than other machines such as cars, planes, and satellites; that is, only a mechanical creature.

This was a great blow to humanity and yet human values were not wholly condemned except in some schools of thought where ideas like peace, freedom, spirituality, justice and compassion were considered as jokes.

Reappearance of Humanity and the Occurred Contradiction

But since the middle of the 19th century, humanity has won fresh attention in philosophical schools Such as schools of humanity and even worship of human beings. In the past the human being was only a sign of spirituality and the Qur'an speaks of the human being as being the worthiest creature through whom God could be understood.

Now the human being is trying to recover its former honor and sanctity and become a goal in itself but without the adoption of the former criteria and without a regard for its divine or non-divine aspect, or the points stated in the Qur'an that everything that is created on earth is for it and that God has breathed some of this spirit into it to making it a manifestation of Himself.

There is no longer any talk of the above matters, nor even a discussion of internal human motives, but only a belief in the sanctity of humanity and its intelligence. Now we see all schools of thought and even the declaration of human rights beginning their claims with respect for the inherent dignity of human beings. They say this in order to base their education on its foundation and though each individual is able to violate the rights of others, this respect for the dignity and sanctity of humanity will serve as a check to such violations.

Most of those who follow the philosophy of humanitarianism, have criteria different from those of the past. But the difficulty lies in this same contradiction in the life, thought and logic of mankind today, a logic which lacks foundation.

Absolute Peace

I do not think that there are any scholars in the world who would interpret humanitarianism to mean universal peace. There are, of course, ordinary people who think all human beings in the world are the same and of equal worth. But this is not true. One is learned, another is ignorant; one is virtuous, another is impure; one is tyrannical, another is oppressed; one is benevolent, another is malevolent. Should we consider them all the same from a humanitarian point of view, irrespective of their knowledge, faith, chastity and benevolence or vice versa?

If we say so, we are betraying humanity. Let me give an

example. Both A and B are human beings who are biologically similar. If you dislike one of them, it has nothing to do with his blood group. But if you are humanitarian, you cannot be indifferent to both of them and claim that they are equally human; for then both should be equally liked, or both equally disliked.

The Fundamental Difference between Man and Animals

But this is not so since the human being's basic difference with animals is that the human being has more potentiality than animals and less actuality. What does that mean? A horse on its birth possesses all the peculiarities that a horse should have and if it has less than that, it can gain it by practice. But a human being has potential only at birth. It is not known what he or she will be in the future. The shape is human hut that person may, in reality, become a wolf or a sheep or a human being.

Mullā Ṣadrā, the great Iranian Islamic philosopher, in pointing out the error of people in thinking human beings equal in everything, says that there are as many kinds of individuals as there are individuals. He is, of courses regarding the human being philosophically, not biologically. A biologist pays attention to human organs and limbs, while a philosopher concentrates on the human being's qualities and thus he cannot believe that human beings are all of the same kind. That is why human values are potential. Some attain the height of humanity while others fail to do so. As Imām ʻAlī (A.S.) says, "The shape is humans but the mind may be a beast."[1] Not all individuals have an interior proportionate to their exterior.

1. Ibid, 119.

The Religion of Humanity "Auguste Comte"

As I said before, to a great extent, the world is returning, once again to the school of humanity, meaning that philosophies of humanity have appeared; and the strangest of them all is the creed of humanity which Auguste Comte originated in the middle of the 19th century. This man wavered between his intelligence and mind on the one hand and his heart and conscience on the other and came to the conclusion that the human being needed a creed, the absence of which results in all kinds of social corruption. According to him, past religion (Catholicism) is not adequate enough for modern mankind. He describes three stages of religion; the divine supernatural stage, the philosophical reasoning stage and the scientific positive stage. He said that Catholicism belonged to the human being's supernatural thinking and this is not acceptable to the person of the scientific age. His invented religion however, lacked an occult root, but he accepted all the traditions and rites which existed before, and even proposed having priests in this new creed, presenting himself as its prophet, but a prophet without a god. They say about him that he got his rites from Catholicism and he was criticized for this since he disbelieved that religion but imitated and adopted its ceremonies and traditions. He was right in one thing, that the human being needs worship and devotion as well as the performance of a number of rites.

He seems to have found a large number of followers in Europe and America and his house has become a center of pilgrimage for them. According to some Arabic books, he had fallen in love with a lady whose husband had been condemned to life imprisonment, but she died before he could win her and consequently he turned away frown the world of the intellect to the world of sentiments and eventually started his creed of humanity. This lady-love is considered by his followers as holy as Mary, the mother of Christ. But this school of humanity underwent a number of changes which gave it its present form.

Man's Freedom and Responsibility

One of the questions concerning the human being is freedom and responsibility. Is the human being really free and independent or does it have a responsibility and a mission to perform? According to the Qur'an, the human being is faced with no compulsion before God. On the contrary, the human being is created a free being with a fixed responsibility and mission. The Holy Qur'an refers to the human being as the vice-gerent of God, while no others Holy book has given such sanctity to the human being.

God says in the Qur'an,

> And when your Lord said to the angels, I am setting on the earth a vice-gerent, they said, What will You set therein one who will do corruption there and shed blood ... But God answered, Assuredly I know what you know not. (2:28)

All that, is evidence of the human being's talents and potentialities. You see, then, that Islam, which is a school of humanity, believes in the exalted position of the human being from a philosophical point of view. The Qur'an says again that God taught the human being the names of all things. Then it showed itself superior to the angels in this knowledge and God reproached the angels for what they did not know about humanity and while they supposed the human being to be a creature of wrath and lust, they had ignored the other side of its character. The angels confessed their ignorance and begged for His forgiveness. Then God told the angels to prostrate themselves before His creature.

The greatest interpretation that can be given to this command in order to show the human being's mission freedom and option is that God makes it the vice-gerent of and the successor to himself. God is the Creator and here He confers some of His creative power on the human being to benefit from.

Man's Happiness and Pleasure

Another question shout the human being is its happiness and pleasure. I say briefly that the human being seeks pleasure. Where should it be found? Is it from within the self or from without, or from both within and without and in what proportion? Those who focus their attention on sures outside themselves, wrongly supposing that the whole joy of life is this, have not been able to know themselves as human beings. They cannot consider the life within themselves as a source of joy and pleasure. Their exhilaration lies in a wine-cup, a cabaret.

How well does Rūmī describe a person addicted to drinking and direct that person to righteousness and away from evil saying?

> You are the symbol of existence, wherefore do you seek annihilation?
> You who are an ocean, what do you intend to become?
> Why do you make yourself indebted to wine?[1]

He continues to say that the human being is the essence and the world is the form. It is equally wrong to reject all external things and go to the other extreme of thinking that all joys must be sought internally. In some poems of Rūmī we come across such an exaggeration when he says:

---

1. Jalāl al-Dīn Muḥammad Mawlawī, *Mathnawī*, Book V, verses 3571-2.

> Consider that the way of pleasure is all from within, not without ,
> And think it foolish to abandon customs and traditions.
> Someone is happy and intoxicated in the corner of prison,
> And another is full of grief in his garden.[1]

He does not mean that all external things should be put aside but, at the same time, it should not be supposed that all joys are found in material things. The self is the center of joy and there should be equilibrium between the internal and external.

There are many things to say about the human being. The school of thought which considers itself human should be able to answer certain questions in order to be accepted as a true human school. The human being was considered as the door of spirituality, that is, one could discover the spiritual work through one's own essence. Spirituality and humanism or religion and humanism are two inseparable matters. We cannot accept one of them and abandon the other.

Contradiction in the School of Humanism

The contradiction which we claim to exist in various genuine humanistic schools lies in this point that when humanity suffered a downfall, however wrongly, namely through a change in the Ptolemaic astronomy, it should not make us doubt the exalted position of the human being as a goal in the course of creation. The human being is the goal of the universe whether the earth is the center of the universe or not. What does the phrase 'goal of the universe' mean? It means that

1. Ibid, Book VI, verses 3420-21.

nature moves in a certain direction in its evolutionary course whether we consider the human being a spontaneously created being or a continuation of other animal species. it makes no difference to this process whether we think it to possess a divine spirit or not.

God has said, 'We have breathed some of Our spirit into him.' (15:29) He has not said that the human being is the race of God. If He had said that the substance of which the human being is made was brought from another world, then the human being would be a lofty and sacred being.

To those of you whose philosophy is humanitarian, we say, is there a sentiment in the human being either called benevolence, goodness or service, or not? If you say there is not, then to attribute Such a quality to the human being would be as meaningless as calling him a stone or an animal. But the human being has the sentiment. What is it? Someone may say the feeling of service in us is a kind of substitution. What does that mean? When we witness something and our humanitarian feeling is supposedly roused to go and instruct, serve and save the oppressed, we are told that if we ponder about it, we as human beings are putting ourselves in their place, thinking of them first as belonging to our group or our group related to them and then we substitute ourselves for them. Then, the feeling of selfishness which makes us defend ourselves is roused to defend the oppressed; otherwise there is no genuine sentiment in the human being to defend an oppressed person directly.

The school of humanity must firstly answer whether such a sentiment exists in the human being or not? We answer that it does on the basis of its being appointed the vice-gerent of God and as the manifestation of divine generosity and benevolence. It means that while the human bring in its Selfishness is duty-bound to show activity for its survival, tile whole of its existence is not selfishness. The human being also has benevolence, humanity, world-building and moral conscience.

Some time ago when I was in Shīrāz, an organization called the Happy Organization was introduced to me consisting of individuals with an internal sentiment and personal faith and a gathering of the deaf and dumb. I visited one of their classes. For us fastidious people it would he exhausting to spend even one hour in such a class and watch them and their strange gesticulations for a remark. Their teacher was a Sayyid who was named after the first son of Imām and he was showing a great deal of interest and sympathy in those children even though his salary was less than an elementary school teacher's, for that organization was short of funds. He taught them how to write and made them understand words with a great expenditure of effort.

What is this sentiment in the human being? It is the manifestation of humanity and its genuineness. Generally speaking, what is this sense of praise for the good and dislike for the sick, even though they belong to the distant past? When we hear the names of Yazīd and Shimr and remember their wickedness and crimes, and on the other hand, when the names of the martyrs of Karbalā are mentioned, we have a feeling of hatred for the first group and a sense of wonder and respect for the latter. What is the reason for it? Is it a class feeling which makes us think of ourselves as belonging to the group of the martyrs of Karbalā and dislike Yazīd and Shimr as we dislike our enemies? Do we project our feelings of sympathy and hatred on to each group respectively, while in truth both are related to ourselves? If this is so then the person you consider your enemy will be no different from you. For in his turn he has the right to praise those you dislike and hate those you praise.

On the contrary you may look upon it from a different angle which is not personal and individual but is related to the whole of humanity in which there is no question of personal dislike but the truth. There your connection with the martyrs in your praise, and your dislike of their enemies, is not personal but general and universal.

The school of humanity must supply an answer to what these feelings are and whence they arise and to such problems as the human being's honest love of gratitude, to someone who has done a good deed. When the genuineness of human values are discovered, then the question of the human being crops up. Is the human being who has such genuine qualities the same person spoken of by materialism? Is that person a machine, a satellite? A machine, however big, is only big, if a machine is made a thousand times bigger than an Apollo, what could we say about it? We could say it is great, amazing and extraordinary but not noble or sacred. Even if it is made a billion times bigger, possessing a billion pieces, again it can only be called amazing and extraordinary but never noble, holy and honorable.

The Relation between Humanism and God

How can the declaration of human rights and communist philosophers who support human genuineness in various forms, speak of the human being's inherent prestige and sacredness without paying attention to God's words saying, 'We breathed some of Our spirit into him.'(15:29) When they ascertain the genuineness of these values then they can realize the genuineness of the human being itself.

Now supposing we realize this genuineness of the human being is it only the human being who exists in this universe which is in infinite darkness? As a European says, is the human being only a drop of sweat in an ocean of poison created accidentally? Or is the human being a drop of sweet water in a sweet ocean? Does this small light represent universal light?

Here the relation of the genuineness of the human being with God will become clear, for both of them are inseparable. In the phrase of the Holy Qur'an, 'God is the light of the heavens and the earth', the word God is not what Aristotle calls the first Cause for that is different from the God of Islam. His god is separate from and foreign to the universe. But the God Of Islam, when the phrase, 'He is the First, He is the Last, He is the Outer and He is the Inner.' (57:3) is heard, it at once gives you a different view of the universe. Then you understand the meaning of all the genuine qualities within yourself and realize that there is a goal. You will see that if you are a beam of light then a whole world of light exists and if you are a drop of sweat water it is because an infinite ocean of sweetness exists there and a ray of His light is within you.

Islam is a humanistic school based on human criteria there is nothing in it based on wrong discriminations between human beings. In Islam there exists no country, race, blood, zone and language. These things are not an evidence and criterion of privilege for human beings. That criterion in Islam is those human values. If it respects those values, it is because it believes in the genuineness of the human being and the universe; that is, it believes in God Almighty. That is why Islam is the only humanistic school that has for its foundation proper logic and there exists no other such school in the world.

Discourse 3
Spiritual Freedom I

> Say, oh people of the Book! Come now to a word common between us and you that we worship none but God and that we associate not aught with Him and do not some of us take others as Lord, apart from God. (3:64)

The subject of our discussion is spiritual freedom. The points that I wish to submit to this gathering tonight are as follows: Firstly, the nature of freedom; secondly, how many kinds of freedom there are though I confine myself to two types here, namely, spiritual freedom and social freedom and thirdly, the relationship between these two types of freedom and the extent to which spiritual freedom is possible without social freedom and vice versa. The discussion will mainly be centered round the last point, namely, the connection between the two types of freedom.

The Term *Mawlā*

I begin my discourse with a point which is relevant to this occasion, the birthday anniversary of Imām ʻAlī, the Master (*mawlā*) of the virtuous. One of the words we often use in connection with his personality is the word master and master of the virtuous and master of the masters. When we quote his sayings we add one of the above epithets instead of his name.

This epithet was first used by the Holy Prophet about him in his famous remark, 'Alī (A.S.) is a master for him who accepts me as his master (when he lifted him up to present him to his followers), an uttering unanimously affirmed by both the *Shiites* and the *Sunnīs.* The word has also appeared in the Holy Qur'an, 'If you both turn to God then indeed your hearts are already inclined (to this); and if you hack up each other against him, then surely God is Who is his Master and Gabriel and the believers that do good, and the angels after that are the aiders.' (66:4)

What does the word master mean? I do not wish to go into great lengths about it tonight but to be brief. The original meaning of it is 'proximity' of two things which are close to one another. Therefore it is sometimes used with two opposite meanings. For example, God is said to be the Master of His servants. It is also used to mean a master or even a slave. Another meaning of it is both liberator and liberated.

In which sense, then, did the Prophet (S)use the word '*mawlā*' in his utterance meaning, "As I am a master and friend to a person, then 'Alī (A.S.) is his master and friend." [1] I have no intention of saying which meaning was, in my opinion, expressed here. But in connection with my discourse I may mention that the poet Jalāl al-Dīn Rūmī has tastefully used the word in his *Mathnawī* and taken it to mean liberator. The word occurs in chapter six of his work in a well-known story of the woman and the treacherous judge. In this story the judge wants to hide in a chest. He is hidden there and the chest is given to a porter to carry. The judge begs the porter with the

1. Muḥammad Bāqir Majlisī, *Biḥār al-Anwār*, vol. 37, 115.

promise of a fine reward to go and find the judge's assistant to come and buy the chest. The assistant comes and buys the chest. Here the poet makes a digression to say, "All of us are confined in the chest of the lustful body without being aware of it and we need liberating prophets and apostles to deliver and save us." Then he goes on to say, It was for this reason that the assiduous Prophet Applied the word Master to himself and 'Alī (A.S.) Saying whoever has me as his master and friend must have 'Alī, my cousin, as his master too. Who is a master? He is one who liberates you and removes the fetters from your legs.

This is really true whether the Prophet's remark, "Whoever has me as his master has 'Alī as his master," would have the same meaning or not, that is, whether he used the word master to mean that he and 'Alī (A.S.) were liberators or not. The fact remains that every rightful Prophet is sent to liberate people and every rightful Imām possesses the same quality.

The Meaning of Freedom and Liberty

Now let us see what is the meaning of freedom and liberty. Freedom is a requisite of life and evolution and one of the greatest needs of living creatures, whether they are plants, animals or human beings. The difference in their freedom lies in their differences of structure. The human being needs a freedom beyond that of plants and animals. Every living thing must grow and find perfection. It cannot remain stationary. Solids do not grow so they have no need of freedom. But living creatures need three things for their growth and evolution: nurturing, security and freedom.

Nurturing consists of a number of factors required by living creatures for their growth. For example, a plant needs soil and water as well as light and heat in order to grow. An animal needs food and other things. A human being's needs are the same as those of plants and animals plus a series of other needs which would come under the heading of nurturing, all of which are like food for it. How can one live without food? The faculty of nourishment is a necessary asset to a living being.

The next requisite of a living being is security. What does security mean? It means being able to keep the means and equipment necessary for living. It should not be withheld from them by an enemy or a foreign power. Next to this nurturing it needs security in order to keep its life and wealth and health and belongings safe against aggression.

The third need is freedom. What does freedom mean? It means the absence of obstacles in the way of growth. For example, in growing a plant, in addition to other requisites, you must provide a suitable environment for it and remove all obstacles. If you plant a tree under a roof, you are depriving it of free space above to attain its full growth. Thus every living being needs freedom for its growth and evolution. What is this freedom? It is the absence of barriers. Free persons are those who fight against all obstacles set in their way of growth and perfection. They do not submit to obstacles.

Kinds of Freedom

Now we must see what types of freedom there are. The human being is a peculiar being and his or her life is a social one, in addition to being a complex creature in his or her individual life. Human beings are quite different from plants and animals; they have certain other needs which may be divided into two kinds. One of them is social freedom. What does social freedom mean? It means having freedom in connection with other individuals in society, so that they do not hinder their growth, do not imprison them to check their activities, do not exploit or enslave them, do not exploit all their physical and mental powers in their own interests. This is called social freedom which may in its turn be of several types.

One of the greatest problems of human beings throughout history has been this same abuse of power by powerful elements in subjugating others and enslaving them so as to enjoy the whole fruits of their lives and labor.

Do you know what exploitation means? It means picking someone else's fruits. For each person his or her essence is a fruitful tree and his or her labor and thoughts are the product of that tree. This crop must be his or hers. But when others seize these fruits by one means or another, we say a person is exploited by another or others. Throughout history one person has been exploited by another person or a people by another people or enslaved by them. Or at least they have been deprived of the opportunity to give the exploiter a greater chance to secure maximum benefits. For example, suppose a piece of land belongs to two men but one of them who is stronger takes possession of the whole land and expels the other or employs him as a laborer; that will be a form of slavery.

Social Freedom in the Qur'an

In the Holy Qur'an, one of the explicit purposes of the prophets has been to offer mankind social liberty and deliver them from their mutual enslavement. The Qur'an is a wonderful Book. Some ideas flourish in a particular period while they lose their brilliance at other times. But the case is different with the Qur'an for its ideas and words possess a permanent lustre and this is something of an epic and miracle. One example of which is this idea of social liberty. I do not believe that you can find a sentence elsewhere or at any time about this matter more lively and surging than what you meet in the Qur'an. It has been unrivaled in all the last three centuries when the motto of philosophers has constantly been liberty. This is the sentence, 'Oh Prophet tell all those who claim to follow a divine book of the past (to the Jews, Christians and Zoroastrians or perhaps even the Sabeans whose name occurs in the Qur'an and to all people who follow a previous divine book) to come and assemble around one tenet and under one banner.' (3:64)

What is this banner? The banner consists of two sentences: The first one is that nothing must be worshipped but the unique God, neither Christ nor any other nor the devil should be worshipped. Only God. The second one is that 'none of us must consider another as his slave or master.' This means the abolition of the order of servitude, the system of exploitation, of the exploiter and exploited, getting rid of inequality and doing away with the right of enslavement. This is not the only verse about this matter in the Holy Qur'an. There are many of them but as I wish to be brief, I will mention a few of them. The Qur'an, quoting Moses in his argument with the Pharaoh, quotes the latter's remarks: 'And you did (that) deed of yours which you did; you are one of the ungrateful.' (26:19) Moses answers, 'And is it a favor of which you remind me that you have enslaved the children of Israel?' (26:22)

The Pharaoh had said to Moses, "You are the man who grew up in our house and at our table and when you grew up you committed the crime of killing a man."(All this was meant to make Moses feel lowly and under obligation.) But Moses answered, "Should I remain silent at your enslavement of my people solely because I have grown up in your house? I have come to save these slaves."

The late Āyatullāh Nā'īnī says in his book *Tanzīh al-ummah*, "Everyone knows that the tribe of Moses never worshipped the Pharaoh as the Egyptians did but as the Pharaoh used them as his slaves, the Qur'an employs the word enslavement as uttered by Moses." We definitely know that one of the aims of the Prophets is to establish social freedom and fight against every form of enslavement and social deprivation.

The world of today, too, considers social freedom as being sacred and if you have read the universal declaration of human rights, you will see that the major cause of all wars, bloodshed and misfortunes in the world is that individuals do not respect the freedom of others. Is the logic of a Prophet so far in accord with modern logic? Is liberty sacred? Yes, it is sacred and very much so.

The Prophet (S) always feared the Umayyads and was worried about their future in connection with the Islamic ummah. So he (according to a successive narration) said, "If the offspring of Ibn 'Aāṣ reach thirty in number, they will consider God's property as their own and God's servant as their own servants and will introduce their own innovations in God's religion."[1]

It is true then that social liberty is sacred.

Spiritual Freedom

Another kind of liberty is spiritual freedom. The difference between the Prophets' school and other human schools is that the Prophets have come to offer spiritual freedom to mankind as well as social freedom, the former having a greater value than anything else. Both social liberty and spiritual freedom

1. F. al-Ṭurayḥī, *Majma' al-Baḥrayn*, vol. 5, 367.

are sacred and the former liberty is not possible without the latter. The trouble with modern human society is that it tries to safeguard social liberty without seeking spiritual freedom. In fact it has not the ability to do so, since spiritual freedom is obtainable only through prophethood and Prophets, and through faith and divine books.

Now let us see what spiritual freedom is. The human being is a complex being with various powers and instincts, with strength, appetites, anger, greed, ambition and love of excess. On the other hand, it has been granted reason, mental and moral conscience. Internally and spiritually the human being may feel the self-free or enslaved. It may be a slave of its greed, lust, anger and love of excess or it may be free of all these vices. As the poet says:

I tell the truth and feel thereby happy;
I am a slave to love and free in both worlds.

A person may be so human that that person is socially free and rejects abjectness and servitude and preserves social liberty so ethically; that person also keeps his or her conscience, spirit and intelligence free. This kind of freedom is called 'self- purification' or 'virtue' in religion.

Dependence of Social Freedom upon Spiritual Freedom

Can human beings have social freedom without spiritual freedom? That is, can they be slaves to their own lust, anger and greed and at the same time respect the freedom of others? Today they say yes and they practically expect each person to be a slave to his or her greed, anger and lust and at the same time to respect social liberty. This is one of the many examples of contradictory ideas from which human society suffers.

Human beings in ancient times had no respect for freedom and trampled upon it. Why? Was it because they were ignorant and so they deprived others of their freedom? Can we say that when they gained wisdom, they found it necessary to respect the freedom of others? Is this similar to the question of illness? Faced with sickness, they could rarely find their accidentally-found drugs effective but now with their increase of knowledge they can afford to discard old treatments and resort to new and efficacious ones.

We wish to know whether the action of ancient people in depriving others of their freedom was solely due to ignorance? No. It had nothing to do with ignorance or knowledge. Human beings were fully aware of their actions which served their interests. Was their lack of respect for the rights of others and liberty due to the forms the law took? If so, could a change of law bring about a change of behavior? For example, did the abolition of slavery in America really put an end to slavery? Or did it only change the form of slavery without changing the context? Was this disregard of the freedom of others due to their way of thinking and their philosophy?

It was none of these; it was nothing but self-interest. As an individual, the human being sought only to secure maximum profit for himself and get benefit from every possible means. Other human beings were one such means for him and he used them in the same way that he used wood, stone, iron and domestic animals. When he planted a tree or cut it down, the last thing that he cared about was the tree itself. He thought only of the way that the tree benefitted him. When he fattened a sheep and then slaughtered it, what was his purpose but self-interest? When he enslaved other human beings and deprived them of their rights, it was to benefit himself. Thus all his actions including trampling on other people's liberty were based on self- interests. Is he the same today? Yes. He is and he has not changed at all. On the contrary, it should be said that his mouth is even opened wider to swallow more.

Neither science nor law has been able to check greed. The only thing they have done is to change the form of it. The content is the same with a new cover. Ancient man was an outspoken being and had not yet reached the state of hypocrisy. When the Pharaoh enslaved people, he frankly declared to Moses, 'What is your answer, Moses? These are my servants and slaves.' (23:48)

The Pharaoh did not hide his deeds of exploitation and enslavement. But today human beings deprive others of all their rights and freedom in the name of a free world and under the pretext of defending peace and liberty. Why is it so? Because human beings lack spiritual freedom and are not virtuous and free in their souls. Imām 'Alī (A.S.) has an utterance about virtue which, like his other sayings, is highly worthy, even though to some people it seems old fashioned. He says, "Divine virtue is the key to every truth, provisions for the resurrection day, factor of release from any sort of slavery and deliverance from any cause of perditions."[1]

The phrase shows that virtue delivers the human being from every kind of servitude and frees him or her spiritually to enable him or her to give freedom to others.

The True Liberal Man

Who, then, is a true liberal in the world? It is men like 'Alī Ibn Abī Ṭālib, (A.S.),who stand in the same rank as he or are

1. Imām 'Alī, *Nahj al-Balāghah*, 351.

trained in his school. For they are, in the first place, liberated from the bonds of self. 'Alī (A.S.), says, "Shall I content myself with being entitled 'Amīr al-Mu'minīn' (the master of the faithful) and how can I oppress anybody for my own sake?"[1]

Only a person who resembles 'Alī (A.S.) can truly be free and generous at all times or is at least his follower and calls his mind and spirit to account. When 'Alī (A.S.) was at the altar of prayer, stroking his beard, he said, "Oh worldly things. Oh gold and silver. Go away and deceive others but 'Alī (A.S.), for he has divorced you forever."[2] Only a person in whose heart and conscience there is a heavenly call can truly have a respect for people's rights and liberty without feeling the slightest hypocrisy. When such a man who possesses such chastity and spirituality and fears God is in a position of governor, he never feels that he is a man of power and other men are subjugated by him. Although custom makes people keep their distance from him, he persuades them not to do so and to come close to him. When 'Alī (A.S.) started his campaign for the battle of Ṣiffīn, he reached the town of Anbar which is now a part of Iraq but was then an old Iranian town. A number of the great citizens such as the mayor and aldermen had come forth to welcome the Caliph in a fitting manner, for they imagined 'Alī (A.S.) to be a royal successor to the Sassanid Kings. The moment he arrived on horseback, they started running towards him. 'Alī (A.S.) called them and asked what they meant by such behavior. They answered that it was their way of showing respect to their kings and great men. The Imām told them not to act thus for it meant abasing themselves before their Caliph. He said, "I am one of you and you are treating me badly by such behavior for you may (God

1. Ibid, 417.
2. Ibid, 480.

forbid) fill me with pride and cause me to consider myself superior to you."[1]

This is what is meant by a generous person who possesses spiritual freedom and has welcomed the call of the Qur'an, 'To worship nothing other than God'. No man or stone or heaven or earth or any human attribute is worthy of worship but God. I will read you a sermon of 'Alī (A.S.) ,so that you may have an idea of his generosity and spirituality.

The sermon is rather long and is related to the mutual rights of the governor and the governed towards one another. 'Alī (A.S.) as a ruler advises his people to feel free with him and not to consider their governors as being superior to themselves. He says, "Do not use for him the expressions they use for tyrants by which they might abase themselves and elevate them." He wants them to speak with him as they do with ordinary people. He says, "If by chance they found him angry and hot-tempered, they should not lose courage, but should freely state their objections."[2] He continues that they should not confirm and express agreement with every word and action of his. He says that they should not suppose their true words to seem to him too heavy to bear. On the contrary, he would be well pleased to hear truth and proper criticism. He goes on to say that even though he is their ruler and Caliph and they are his subjects, they should not praise and flatter him. Then he lays down a general principle by saying that a man who cannot bear hearing truth will find it even more difficult to act truly.

Christensen writes that Anūshīravān, the Sāsāniyān King, had assembled a number of people to discuss a matter. He

---

1. Ibid, 334-335.
2. Ibid.

stated his own opinion and everyone agreed with it. A secretary present, supposing this gathering to be a truly group discussion was duped into asking permission to express his own view. He did so and criticized the King's opinion. The King angrily called him insolent and at once ordered him to be punished. They knocked him so much on the head with his own pen box that he died.[1]

In conclusion, 'Alī (A.S.) makes a request. He begs them never to withhold their true words and objections and counsels from him.

This is an example of a perfect man who is spiritually free while he enjoys the rank of a ruler and in this way he grants social liberty to others. I pray God to make us a follower of 'Alī (A.S.).

---

1. Arthur Christense, *L'Iran sous les sassanides* (*Iran dar Zamān Sāsāniyān*).

Discourse 4
Spiritual Freedom II

> And removes from them their burden and the shackles which were upon them. (7:157)

Last week I mentioned that our discussion consists of three parts: The meaning of freedom, the two kinds of freedom, namely social and spiritual freedom and the dependence of these two types of freedom upon one another, especially the dependence of social freedom on spiritual freedom.

Tonight, I wish to devote myself to the subject of spiritual freedom, its meaning and its necessity for mankind. This is particularly urgent since today little attention seems to be paid to spiritual freedom by human societies, which is the cause of many present troubles. This is so evident that many people consider spiritual freedom as something abolished, even though the need for it is much greater than in the past. What does spiritual freedom mean? Freedom requires two sides so that one side becomes free of the bond of the other. In spiritual freedom what must the human be free of? Spiritual freedom is freedom from one's self as against social freedom which is freedom from the bonds of others. One may be asked whether the human being can be enslaved by the self.

Can a person be both a slave and a slave owner? The answer is in the affirmative. In the case of animals this may not be true but what about this strange being called the human being? How is it possible for it to be at the same time a slave and master?

Man: A Complex Existent

The reason is that the human being is a complex creature and that is a fact which has been confirmed by religion and philosophy by scientists and psychologists and about which no doubt exists.

Let me begin by an interpretation of the Qur'an on Creation which says, 'So when I have shaped him and breathed into him of My spirit, fall you down, bowing before him.' (15:29)

It is not necessary to know what this divine spirit means, but it is enough to know that this earthly being is granted something else which is unearthly. According to a Tradition, the Prophet (S) says that God created angels and granted them only intelligence. He created animals and gave them only appetites and He created man and granted him both intelligence and appetite; an utterance of the Prophet (S) that has been used in a poem by Rūmī. Now, besides these verses of the Qur'an and Traditions and what has been affirmed by philosophers and psychologists, what does spiritual freedom consist of in simple language. We will begin with something which everyone would understand.

Slavery of the Spirit

Undoubtedly we need food to live and the more of it the better, and we need clothing and the finer the better and we require a dwelling and the more magnificent the better. We desire wives and children, luxury, money and material things. But at one point we may reach a cross- road where we should keep our honor and nobility and at the same time put up with poverty, eat dry bread, wear shabby clothes, live in a poor hut and have no money and be distressed. If we ignore our honor and nobility and submit to abjection, then all material benefits will be provided for us. We see that many people are not willing to suffer abasement for the sake of material things while others readily accept this exchange, even though they and their consciences are ashamed of themselves.

In the *Gulistān*, Sa'dī describes two brothers, one of whom was rich and the other poor. The former was in the service of the government and the latter was an ordinary worker who secured a livelihood by manual labor. One day the rich brother said to his poor brother, "Why don't you accept government service, to be delivered from hardship and distress?" The poor brother answered, "Why don't you work to be delivered from abjection?"[1]

That kind of service with all its accompanying wealth means lack of freedom, for, it involves bowing to others and being humbled. Sa'dī goes on to say that according to the wise, sitting down to eat your own bread is far better than wearing a golden belt and standing to serve others.

You may be well-versed about this subject but I wish you to analyze it from a psychological point of view. What feeling makes the human being prefer pain and hardship, labor and poverty to humbling himself or herself before others? He calls it captivity to serve others though it is not of the type of

1. Shaykh Muṣliḥ al-Dīn Sa'dī, *Gulistān*, Bāb 1. Ḥikāyat 36.

material slavery. It is not his or her strength that is enslaved but the spirit. There is a quatrain attributed to ʻAlī (A.S.), saying, "If you desire to live freely, labor like a slave, work and suffer pain and shut your eyes from Adam's offspring whoever they may be, even from Ḥātam Ṭā'ī (a heroic figure famous for his generosity in pre-Islamic Arabia). So have no expectation not only from mean people but also from the generous."

He goes on to say that when a job is offered to someone, that person considers it below his or her dignity to accept it. He or she thinks every kind of manual labor as mean. But ʻAlī (A.S.), believes that every kind of work and labor is better than extending your hand before others begging for something. He says, "Nothing is worse than going to others to beg for something."

Having no need of others means being superior to them. Once I came across a remark of the poet Ḥāfiẓ who was an extraordinarily eloquent man and had a deep respect for ʻAlī (A.S.). He quotes nine sayings of his which are relevant to our discussion, one of which is, "You may be in need but remember that if you have need of someone, you still turn yourself into his slave. But if you do away with that need, you will be his equal and if you show benevolence to someone, you will be his master."

Slavery with regard to the Wealth

So you see that your need makes you someone's slave What kind of slavery? Slavery of spirit. These sayings are fine but today they are disregarded since mankind prefers to discuss other problems and pays little attention to ethical ones.

Again ʻAlī says, "Greed means perpetual slavery." Thus he considers greed worse than slavery. Here then, spiritual slavery is mentioned as something worse than physical slavery.

There is also slavery to wealth against which all moralists have warned mankind.

Another saying of ‘Alī is, "The world is a passage not a residence." Again he says, "There are two groups of people in the world." He continues, "One of these two groups come and sell and enslave themselves and go and the others come and buy their freedom and go." These two attitudes can also be applied to wealth, either to be a slave of wealth or free from it. A person should say that as he or she must not be a slave to riches, he or she should say, "I am a human being. Why should I make myself a slave of inanimate things like gold and silver, land and other things?"

But the truth is that when a person thinks the self to be a slave of wealth, that person is in fact a slave to his or her mental characteristics, a slave to greed and one's animal nature. For inanimate things like money, land, machine and even animals have no power to enslave that person. When one ponders deeply over this matter, one finds the source of slavery to lie in one's own peculiarities such as greed, lust, anger and carnal desires.

The Qur’an says, ‘Have you noticed someone who 11as made his carnal desires his god?’ Wealth itself is not to blame when a person is warned against his or her own desires. Thus if one liberates oneself from the bond of one's wicked desires, one will realize that one is not at the service of wealth.

It is then that one finds one's own true worth and understands the significance of this verse of the Qur’an, ‘All We have created on the earth is for you.’ (2:29) Thus riches are at the service of the human being and not vice versa. If so, then, envy and avarice have no meaning and if one engages in them, one is enslaving oneself. There are two stages for the human being: A lower, animal stage and a higher, human one.

The Prophets are sent to preserve the spiritual freedom of humanity. What does that mean? It means preventing human honor, humanity, intelligence and conscience from being subjugated to its own lust, passion and love of profits. If you overcome your passion, you are free. If you conquer your lust and not vice versa, you are free.

If you are in a position to gain an illegitimate profit, but your faith and conscience and intelligence forbid you to do so, you have overcome your desire and then you can say that you are really spiritually free.

If you see a woman, but you check your lustful desires and obey your conscience, then you are a free human being. But if your eyes, ears, and stomach incite you to satisfy them by whatever means, then you are their slave.

Human Ego and Animal Ego

The human being is ruled by two types of ego: An animal ego and a human one. This fact and this contrast are well illustrated by Rūmī in a story of Majnūn (in eastern literature, Majnūn is the equivalent of Romeo and Laila is the equivalent of Juliet) and the camel.

The story goes that Majnūn was riding a camel intending to visit Lailā's home. The camel happened to have a baby camel and Majnūn, in order to ride faster to his destination, confined the baby camel to the house. He was deep in thought about his Beloved while the camel was worried about its young. Every moment Majnūn absentmindedly let the reins loose, the camel turned back towards home. This was repeated several times until the camel collapsed. The poet digresses to say that the human being has two kinds of inclinations: that of the spirit and that of the body.

If you wish to be free in spirit, you cannot be a glutton, a woman-worshipper, a money-lover, a lustful person of passion. I have come across a narrative in the *Nahj al-Balāghah* which says that one day the Prophet (S) went among the Companions (the *Anṣār* who were the poor followers of the Prophet (S) in Medina who had migrated there. The Prophet (S)first let them stay in a mosque, but a divine command was issued to him to find another home for them since a mosque was not a proper place to live in and they obeyed the order. Subsequently, they lived in a large shelter near the mosque). One of them said to the Prophet, "I feel as if the whole world is worthless in my eyes." He did not mean that he made a similar use of stones and gold but that neither of them had the power to attract him. The Prophet (S) looked at him and said, *" Now I can say that you are free."* [1]Thus we can say that spiritual freedom is in itself something real.

Man Judging Himself

We can give other reasons to show that the human being's personality is complex and that one can either be spiritually free or a slave. God Almighty has granted this power to a person to be one's own judge. In society, a judge stands apart from the plaintiff and defendant. Have you ever heard a person to be his own plaintiff and defendant and judge, all at the same time?

A person is called just. What is a just human being? Does it not mean that a person can judge impartially about one's own

---

1. Ibn Abī'l-Ḥadīd, *Sharḥ Nahj al-Balāghah*, vol. 11, 215.

problems and issue a verdict against one when guilty? Does this not show the complex nature the human being? Many a time you have seen people who judge fairly about themselves and prefer the rights of others to their own. The late Sayyid Ḥusain Kūh Kamarī who was a great religious authority with a following and an uncle o the late Āyatullāh Ḥujjat Kūh Kamarī who was our teacher was such a man. It is narrated about him that he had theological class in Najaf which had not yet won the reputation it had later on, especially as his stay in Najaf had not been long for he had been in the habit of travelling here and there to benefit from the teachings of the great masters in various towns such as Mashhad, Iṣfahān and Kāshān.

The late Shaykh Anṣārī who was dressed poorly and whose eyes suffered from trachoma happened to teach in the same mosque as Sayyid Ḥusain, each in turn, the Shaykh first and Sayyid Ḥusain next, without meeting each other. One day the latter happened to arrive an hour earlier than usual. As there was no time to go home and come back, he thought he would wait there for his pupils to arrive. He noticed a peculiar looking Shaykh sitting there teaching two or three fellows. He sat in a corner and could hear the Shaykh's words. He found them to be profound and wise. It was a strange experience for a great scholar like him to meet an unknown but erudite teacher. He decided to go earlier to the mosque once more to see how things went. The second visit proved to be as beneficial as the first and he found the Shaykh very learned and in fact more of a scholar than himself. On repeating the experience for the third time, he was fully convinced of the man's profound knowledge. So he decided to join the small class and when his own pupils arrived, he said to them,"I have news for you. That Shaykh is much more learned than I am as I have discovered and I advise you to accompany me to join his class." They arose together and attended the Shaykh's class.

What is the implication of such fairness? Sayyid Ḥusain turned himself into a pupil of Ansari and gave up his claim to being an authority. He must have felt, as we do, what respect and mastership are and must have been pleased at being an authority. And yet his noble and free spirit allowed him to judge fairly between himself and that man, and issue a verdict against himself. This is proof of the human being's complex personality.

The Conscience Blames

A person commits a sin and then blames the self. What is this prick of conscience? Exploiting governments train individuals in such a way as to kill their conscience . And yet when that conscience is supposed to be dead, a small light is noticed to scatter its beams at its proper time. The pilot of the plane who bombed Hiroshima was actually trained for such a crime but when he dropped his bomb and saw the city burning and the innocent men and women and children who had no connection with war, being annihilated, he felt spiritually sick. In America they gave him a fine welcome but they could not check that torture of conscience which led him eventually to a lunatic asylum. The Qur'an says, 'Nay, I swear by the Self- reproaching soul ...' (75:2)

Imām Ṣādiq (A.S.) says, "He who is not granted a preacher within himself by God, will not be affected by other's preaching."[1] Do not deceive yourself into thinking that you will be influenced by others if you are not influenced by your own conscience. One of our religious injunctions is to judge ourselves and issue a verdict against ourselves when necessary. 'Call yourself to account before you are called to account.'

1. Ḥusain Nūrī al-Tabrisī, *Mustadrak al-Wasā'il wa Mustanbaṭ al-Masā'il*, vol. 11, 140.

'Weigh yourself before you are weighed for your deeds on the Day of Resurrection .'[1]

All these show the human being's complex personality which has a lower animal side and higher human side. Spiritual freedom means that the higher side is free from the lower one.

Man Punishes Himself

In connection with self-punishment, I remember a case related to Imām 'Alī. A man came to him to repent, supposing that by saying the sentence of repentance, everything would be all right. 'Alī reprimanded him sharply by saying, "May your mother mourn for you. Do you know what repentance means? It is very much higher than saying a sentence."[2] Then he told the man that repentance is based on several things: Two principles, two conditions of acceptance and two conditions of completion. That is, a total of six points.

He then explained this by saying, "The first principle is that one should be truly penitent of one's past wicked deeds. The second is to decide never to commit that sin in the future. The third is to grant people their right if one owes it to them. The fourth is to perform the obligatory devotions which one may have forsaken."[3] The last two points, 'Alī mentioned are most relevant to my discourse. They are: Fifthly, to melt down the flesh that is grown on you by lustfulness through sorrow and constant grief; and lastly, to give this body which has in the past been addicted to the pleasure of sin, the pain of worship and devotion.

---

1. Al-Ḥurr al-'Āmilī, *Wasā'il al-Shī'ah*, vol. 16, 99.
2. Imām 'Alī, *Nahj al-Balāghah*, 549.
3. Ibid.

Have there been people in the past who have reached this stage? Yes. There have. Today we may forget that repentance exists. But we can cite a fine example of it by mentioning Mullā Ḥusain Qulī Hamadānī who was a great moralist of modern times and a pupil of the great religious scholars, the later Mīrzā Shīrāzī and Shaykh Anṣārī. A sinful man goes to him to be guided. When the man came back after a few days, he could hardly be recognized due to his extraordinary leanness. The Mullā used neither a whip nor a weapon nor a threat. But he could offer true spiritual guidance. He managed to awaken that man's conscience to fight his lust and passion.

Spiritual Freedom, Prophets' Greatest Plan

The most significant program of the prophets is to provide spiritual freedom. Self- purification is in fact spiritual freedom. The Qur'an says, 'Prosperous is he who purifies it and failed has he who seduces it.' (91:9-10)

The greatest damage of our time is speaking of freedom and confining it to social freedom. Spiritual freedom is never spoken of and, in consequence, social freedom is not secured. A great crime is committed in our time in the form of philosophy and philosophical schools totally ignoring the human being, its personality, spiritual honor and God's revelation, 'I breathed into him of My Spirit,' (15:29) is quite forgotten. They deny that the human being has two aspects an animal side and a human one. They claim that this human being is no different from animals and is subject to the survival of the fittest. This means that each individual' effort is for his or her own interests. Can you imagine how much damage this attitude has done to humanity? They say that life is a battle and the world a battlefield. They also say that a right is what one seizes, not what one ,rants. But the truth is that a right must both be taken and given and not only something which is snatched by force.

The prophets did not come to make such a statement that a right must be seized by force. They came to persuade the oppressed to secure their rights. They also compelled the oppressor to rise against their evil deeds and grant others their rights.

In conclusion I pray God to liberate us all from our carnal desires as he has done for truly generous beings; and to grant us social freedom and blessings in this and the next world; to acquaint us with the facts of Islam; to meet our legitimate needs and to grant salvation to our deceased ones.

Discourse 5
Nobility and Magnanimity of Spirit

> Oh soul at peace return unto your Lord, well pleased, well-pleasing. Enter among My servants. Enter My paradise. (89:28-30)

On the holy birthday anniversary of Imām Ḥusain(A.S.)last Monday I began a discourse saying that anyone who possessed a lofty spirit must suffer physical discomfort while only those who have loose spirits live in comfort, sleep soundly and enjoy delicious dishes and other benefits.

Tonight, I wish to discuss the greatness and nobility of the spirit and show the differences between the two. Greatness of spirit is one thing but nobility is a higher quality. In other words, every greatness is not nobility but every nobility is also greatness.

Great Ambition in the way of Knowledge

Determination is obviously a sign of greatness of the spirit and there are different levels of determination. One person is content to secure a diploma while another knows no limit to the pursuit of knowledge, and his aim is to make the utmost use of his life and gain as much knowledge as he can.

You may have heard the well-known story of Abū Rayḥān al-Bīrūnī, a man whose true worth according to scholars, is not quite known. He was so extraordinary a mathematician, sociologists and historian that he is considered by some to be superior to Ibn Sīnā (Avicenna).

These two were contemporaries. Abū Rayḥān was in love with knowledge, research and discoveries. Sulṭān Maḥmūd summoned him to attend his court and he had to obey the call. He accompanied the King in his conquest of India and found a great treasure of knowledge in that country. But he did not know Sanskrit, so he began learning it. In spite of his old age, he learned it to a very high degree and after many years of study, he produced a book called *Taḥqīq-e mā lil-Hind min maqūlah maqbūlah fi'l-aql aw mardhūlah*, which is a very valuable source of reference for the Indianologists of the world.

He was on his death bed when a jurisprudent neighbor of his, learning of his serious illness, went to visit him. Abū Rayḥān was still conscious and, in seeing the jurisprudent, asked him a question of jurisprudence concerning inheritance or some other issue. The jurisprudent was amazed that a dying man should show interest in such matters. Abū Rayḥān said, "I should like to ask you which is better, to die with knowledge or without it?" The man said, "Of course it is better to know and die." Abū Rayḥān said, "That is why I asked my first question." Shortly after the jurisprudent reached home, the cries of lamentation told him that Abū Rayḥān had died. This shows his determination even at the moments of death.

Great Ambition of Gaining Wealth

One person is great in gathering wealth, for example, while others show no such endeavors and are content with earning a simple livelihood by whatever means they can, whether it is by serving others or begging or submitting to abasement. Are those two types of effort equal? Not at all.

Sometimes you see the people who lack the resolution to get rich, simply because they are weak and others scorn and laugh at them. They recite verses of the Qur'an about asceticism, based on fallacious reasoning. But they are wrong. The person who pursues the amassing of wealth, with all his misery, with all his devotion to the world, is still better than those having a weak determination or no determination, who resemble beggars and thus, he has more character. This person is not blameworthy before him.

These persons can be considered blameworthy only before a real ascetic who himself is a man of determination. Like 'Alī (A.S.) he can gather riches, not because of his own needs, but to spend on others and help the needy. He is in a position to reproach another for whom storing and hiding riches have become a goal, not a means.

Being Overambitious

Similarly, one may seek high rank and position. Alexander the Great was such a man who desired to rule the world. He is a superior to a man who lives in servility and has no determination for feelings of nobility. Nādir Shāh is another example of high- mindedness. These men have great spirits but it cannot be said that they have noble spirits.

Alexander is an example of a great ambition, and his greatness has developed only in one direction, in ambition, fame and influence, in being the most powerful man in the world.

His spirit is noble only to that extent. But did he experience any ease and comfort? Could Nadir have had an easy life with his tyranny, and his building of minarets with the skulls of those he had killed, the man who pulled men's eyes out of their sockets, the man who was madly ambitious? He had no time sometimes to take off his boots for ten days. A story is told about him that in a very severe winter night he reached a caravan serai by himself. The keeper was awakened by a loud knock, and when he opened the gate he saw a burly-looking man riding a big horse. He asked the keeper what food he had, and the latter said he only had eggs.

He was sharply ordered to fry the eggs and bring it with some bread for him and some fodder and barley for his horse. The keeper did so and the man rested there an hour or two and after grooming his horse, he threw some gold coins on to the keeper's lap and said, "Very soon a column of soldiers will reach here. Tell them Nadir has gone in that direction and they must follow at once." On hearing the name of Nadir, the keeper was so frightened that he let the coins fall down. Nadir ordered him to go on the roof and shout to the soldiers on their arrival not to linger a moment but to follow him speedily. The men grumbled when they heard the message but none of them dared to stay a minute to refresh himself.

One may become a Nadir, but he can never enjoy a comfortable bed, fine food and hundreds of other luxuries. His body can never relax. And eventually he will die. Whoever has great determination, in whatever area it may be, will have no physical ease. But none of these men possessed noble souls. Their souls were great but were not noble. Suppose a man to be a great man of learning without any other good quality. He has lofty thoughts about human knowledge. Another is skillful in gathering wealth. Someone else is full of rancour, envy or ambition. All of them are extremely selfish but none of them is noble and magnanimous.

Graciousness

The point is that from a psychological and philosophical point of view, there is another kind of greatness which does not depend on selfishness and which is called humanity.

I have not yet seen how materialists explain away this aspect of the human being. What makes the human being or, at least, some individuals have a feeling of honor in their spirits, something which is beyond and above selfishness? Such a human being wishes to be noble and great, but not at the expense of another. One's spirit does not allow one to tell a lie. Nobility is the opposite of baseness and a person avoids baseness completely.

Mussolini, the well-known Italian dictator, is reported to have said to a friend that he preferred to live like a lion for one year, rather than like a sheep for a hundred years. He insisted that his friend should not quote his words to anyone since his being a lion must mean that other people are sheep and if other people learned what Mussolini desired, they, too, would want to be lions in which case the dictator could no longer remain a lion. There is no nobleness in such an attitude.

But what is a noble person like? It is a person who wants all people to be lions rather than sheep in the world.

The Holy Prophet's Words

The Prophet (S) has said, "I was appointed to perfect the

morality of nobility,"[1] not "I was appointed to perfect good morals." The latter is not the correct meaning. Every innovator of a school claims that what he teaches is right. Even Nietzche who believes in might and has no compassion for the weak, considers his school as one of the true ethics. His words mean nobleness not mastery over others.

Imām 'Alī's Words

'Alī (A.S.) says to his son, Imām Ḥasan (A.S.)"Uplift your spirit above every mean act and think that your spirit is worthier than to be polluted by meanness."[2] He advises his son to think himself nobler than to demean himself by lies or by abasing himself before others. 'Alī (A.S.) says that an honorable person never commits adultery and this is irrespective of the fact that it is forbidden by the divine law and punishable in both worlds. In the epic of the *Nahj al-Balāghah* it is said that in the first encounter of 'Alī (A.S.) with Mu'āwiyah, in the Battle of Ṣiffīn, the Imām had no desire to fight and wished to settle matters through letters and emissaries. But when Mu'āwiyah seized the access to the waters of the Euphrates to prevent 'Alī's army from reaching it, hoping to inflict defeat on them through lack of water, he wrote a letter asking Mu'āwiyah to desist from such strategy since fighting had not begun yet and there was the possibility of reaching an agreement.

Mu'āwiyah refused to forego his advantage and when 'Alī found that his insistance was of no avail, he gathered his men and delivered a discourse saying, "These people are seeking war like food. If so, do you know what should be done? You are

1. Mullā Muḥsin al-Fayḍ al-Kāshānī, *al-Maḥajjat al-Bayḍā' fī Tahdhīb al-Iḥyā'*, vol. 4, 121.
2. Imām 'Alī, *Nahj al-Balāghah*,401.

thirsty and there remains only one way, and that is to quench your swords with their blood in order to satisfy yourselves. If you die victoriously, you are alive but if you live in defeat, you are dead."[1]

This is how 'Alī (A.S.) inspired the spirit of nobility and self-respect in his followers. 'Alī (A.S.) believes that all vices are caused by the baseness of character. For example, he thinks slandering is the act of a weak person.[2] A brave person is so noble and magnanimous that he or she expresses the objections he or she feels for another to that person's face or at least keeps silent. One who is covetous towards others is making the self-contemptuous. One who laments one's misfortune before others is abasing the self.

Someone came before Imām Ṣādiq (A.S.)lamenting his distress and poverty. The Imām asked an attendant to go and pay him a few dinars. The man said in apology to the Imām, "I did not intend to ask for anything." The Imām said, "I did not say that you did but my advice to you is to abstain from narrating your difficulties before others, for you lose your worth, and Islam does not wish a believer to be humbled before others."

'Alī (A.S.) says, "He who describes his helplessness for others is destroying his self-respect and honor which are the dearest things for a true believer. And he who lets his carnal desires dominate him is abasing himself."[3] 'Alī (A.S.) believes that all virtues are due to the nobleness of spirit. Being truthful, honest, perseverant and avoiding all vices are the result of that nobleness. Drinking, to give an example, causes drunkenness,

1. Ibid, 88-89.
2. Ibid, 556.
3. Ibid, 469.

even though temporarily robbing one of reason and reducing one to the level of a stupid animal.

He also says, "I do not base my life on excess."[1]

Damages of Ṣūfīs' Teachings

The teachings of our gnostics and Ṣūfīs have many exalted thoughts. But one of the problems that Islam suffered through the teachings of the gnostics and Ṣūfīs was that it was influenced by the teachings of Christianity, Buddhism and Manicheanism. They lost hold of the correct balance in what they called forgetting the self and killing the self. If they had paid attention to Islam, they would have realized that Islam is in favor of annihilating one aspect of the self and reviving another aspect of it. It advises you to forget your animal self and strengthen your noble spirit. I have come across the same idea in the works of the poet-philosopher, Iqbal Lahouri.

Islam believes that one of the divine punishments is that the human being is brought to forget the self altogether. The Qur'an says:

> Be not one of those who forgot God and so He caused them to forget their souls. (59:19)

Do you know of anyone like 'Alī who called people to renounce the world? 'Alī did this but at the same time he emphasized self-respect and magnanimity. He says to his son, Ḥasan(A.S.)"Do not be the slave of another being. God has created you free."[2] How is it that 'Alī (A.S.) as the most humble

1. Ibid, 546.
2. Ibid, 401.

man in the world, invites people to regard the self? This self that he respects is the noble side of mankind.

We have in hand many sayings of this kind belonging to 'Alī (A.S.) but few quotations from his two sons, a result of the despotic conditions of their time.

Imām Ḥusain's Words

But in the books containing the words of Imām Ḥusain(A.S.)the question of narrowness of the spirit is noticed abundantly, particularly his sayings in the last moments before his martyrdom, blaming those who had sold themselves to tyrants. He says, "If you are not religious and do not fear the Resurrection, at least be free men in your world."[1] In his discourse in Mecca, he says that his spirit does not allow him to live and see such corrupt conditions, let alone be a part of it. Again he says, "Verily I consider death to be nothing but felicity and life with these tyrants to be anything but misery."[2] By this he means that it is an honor for him not to be amongst such people who bring nothing but weariness and sorrow to his soul.

To those who advised him to abandon his fight against tyrants, he quoted the sentence of one of the Prophet's friends, said as an answer to his cousin who wished to prevent him from fighting. The sentence is, "No. I will go forth. Death is no disgrace but honor for a free man whose intention is to follow the right path and fight a holy war. Death in aiding the good and opposing the wicked is an honor." He continues saying,"You who forbid me this humility is enough for you to live in abjection. Do you not see that they do not act according

1. Sayyid Ibn Ṭāwūs, *Luhūf 'alā Qatlā al-Ṭufūf*, 120.
2. Ibid, 79.

to what is right and no one forbids all this corruption?" Again he says, "A believer must seek death."[1] When it was reported to ʻAlī that Muʻāwiyah's army had plundered the town of Anbār, and seized the earnings of a Muslim woman, he says, "By God, if a Muslim dies in sorrow for such a happening, he is not blameworthy."

On the day of his martyrdom (the 10th of Muḥarram), Imām Ḥusain(A.S.)gives this answer to the messenger of Ibn Ziyād who was demanding allegiance, "I will never offer my hand in humiliation nor confess like a slave (that I have been in error)."[2] Even in his last moments of fighting when all his relatives and companions died and he himself, in facing death, and his household is in danger of capture, he continues to declare his exalted goal of nobility and freedom.

Thus we see that all great men are not noble but all noble ones are great. About Imām Ḥusain(A.S.)we must say that he was great in his good deeds, his indifference to wealth, his endeavours in enjoining to good and forbidding the wrong, in his lack of ambition and vengefulness, in his insistence on prayer and communion with God and in his revival of the noble self in fighting for (God and the truth. I pray God to grant us such spirits of nobleness and to give us the awareness of our destiny.

---

1. Ibid.

2. Muḥammad Bāqir Majlisī, *Biḥār al-Anwār*, vol. 45, 37.

Discourse 6
Worship and Prayer I

We sometimes notice points in our Islamic interpretations that raise questions for some of us in connection with worship. For example we are told in the case of prayer that either the Prophet (S) or the Imāms have said, "Prayer is the pillar of religion,"[1] or if we think of religion as a tent, 'prayer is the pole that keeps it standing." This remark is also quoted from the narrations attributed to the Prophet, "The requisite for the acceptance of other human deeds is the acceptance of prayer".[2] In other words, the good deeds of the human being will be null and void if prayer is incorrect and thereby unacceptable.

Another Tradition says, "Prayer is the means of proximity of every virtuous being to God."[3] Another Tradition says that the devil is always uneasy with a believer and shuns him who is devoted to his prayer. The Qur'an, too, shows the remarkable importance of prayer in many verses.

But sometimes it is stated by some persons that all these traditions about prayer must be forged and unreliable and

---

1. Al-Ḥurr al-'Āmilī, *Wasā'il al-Shī'ah*, vol. 4, 27.
2. Ibid, 108.
3. Imām 'Alī, *Nahj al-Balāghah*, 494.

uttered not by the Prophet (S) and his successors but by some devotees in order to win more followers particularly in the 2nd and 3rd centuries of the hegira when the matter of worship had gone to such excess that it had more or less led to monasticism and Sufism.

An Example of Excessiveness in performing Acts of Worship

We see that some people concentrated all their efforts on acts of worship to such an extent that they ignored other religious duties. For example there was among 'Alī's companions a man called Rabī' Ibn Ḥusain, who was later known as Khwājah Rabī' whose tomb is in Mashhad. He was known as one of the eight famous ascetics of the Islamic world and he went so far in asceticism and devotion that he had dug his own grave long before his death. (It is said that for twenty years he never spoke a word about worldly matters). Sometimes he went and lay in it reminding himself that the grave was his home. The only words he was ever heard to say besides prayer was on the occasion of hearing of Imām Ḥusain's martyrdom. He said, "Woe upon these people who murdered the dear descendant of their Prophet." It is reported that afterwards he repented having uttered a sentence other than the invocation of God.

He was a warrior in the time of 'Alī (A.S.) and one day he came to Imām 'Alī and said that they had doubts about that war they were fighting, as it seemed to them to be unlawful, for they were fighting against those who in their prayer turned their faces to Mecca and uttered the formulas of the Islamic creed. This man at the same time did not want to abandon 'Alī (A.S.) so he asked to be given a task in which there was no doubt.

'Alī (A.S.) agreed and sent him to a frontier again as a soldier so that in case of fighting he would face non-Muslims or idolaters. This man was a type of ascetic of the time but of what worth was his asceticism and worship? It is useless to be the follower of a man like ʻAlī (A.S.) and at the same time have doubts about the way shown by him in a holy war. Sometimes people use the phrase, "Why should one observe a fast based on doubt and uncertainty? It is worthless." Islam requires insight combined with practice but Khwājah Rabīʻ had no insight. He lived in the time of Muʻāwiyah and his son Yazīd. He had nothing to do with the social problems of the Islamic society and he used to retire to a corner praying day and night and uttering nothing but the Name of God and regretting his own remark about the martyrdom of Imām Ḥusain (A.S.).

This kind of thing does not accord with Islamic teachings and as the saying goes, "An ignorant person either goes too fast or too slowly."[1]

Excessiveness in the consideration of Social Problems

Some may say that the phrase, "Prayer is the pillar of religion," is not in harmony with Islamic teachings since Islam pays more attention to social matters than any other. Islam says, ‘God orders to do justice and benevolence.’ (16:92) ‘We sent our prophets with manifestations and the Book and justice to make people do justice also.’ (57:25) It commands people to direct others to goodness and forbid evil (3:110) Islam as a great religion is the creed of activity and work. If these matters are important in Islam, then acts of worship and devotion are not so significant. Thus, according to such people, one should follow social teachings and leave acts of devotion and prayer to idle people who have no other task to perform.

---

1. ʻAbd al-Wāḥid al-Āmudī, *Ghurar al-Ḥikam wa Durar al-Kalim*, 479.

But such thoughts are wrong and very dangerous. Islam should be recognized as it is. I emphasize this point since I feel that our society is suffering from a sickness. Unfortunately those who have religious ardor are two groups: One group follow the way of Rabī‘ and think of Islam only as a creed for prayers, hymns and pilgrimage and refer to certain standard books of theology to guide them. They have nothing to do with the world or social regulations or Islamic principles and education.

The reaction to the slowness of this group is the appearance of a second group who go too fast and move on the path of excess. They pay all their attention to social matters, which in itself is a worthy attitude, but ignore acts of worship. I have met people who can well afford to go on a pilgrimage to Mecca, an injunction which is regarded as an important matter in Islam. They ignore prayers, and put aside the matter of imitating a religious leader. They believe that problems related to acts of worship should be solved by oneself, without the need of the guidance of others. Thus everyone is assumed to be a religious expert or a jurisprudent. One is one's own physician and has no need of consulting a doctor or a specialist. There are some who are slack in fasting and its conditions in the case of permanent residence or on a journey and do not believe in making amends for failure to perform acts of worship in their proper time and place.

Both groups consider themselves Muslims but they are not wholly so. Islam does not agree with the phrase, "To believe in some things and disbelieve in other things."79It cannot agree with the acceptance of worship coupled with the rejection of its moral and social questions, or vice versa. You notice that whenever the Qur'an says, ‘Perform your ritual prayer,’ it is followed by, ‘Pay your alms.’

The first injunction concerns the relation between a creature and God and the second one shows the relation between one creature and others. Thus a true Muslim has a dual responsibility towards God and towards human beings and to their society in a permanent way. No Islamic society can be built without worship and invocation of God and prayer and fasting. In the same way, no pious society can exist without directing to goodness and forbidding evils and without kindly relations between individuals, even though a person may be a pious individual.

‘Alī (A.S.) the Perfect Example of Islam

We see ‘Alī (A.S.) as the most exalted, pious man, so much so that his worship was proverbial, a worship full of terror and love and tears. After his death, a man called Ḍirār, who was a companion of his, met Mu‘āwiyah who asked him to describe ‘Alī (A.S.) for him. Ḍirār narrated something he had witnessed about ‘Alī(A.S.). He said, "One night I saw him in his special worshipping place of worship.' He was twisting with the fear of God like a man bitten by a snake and weeping with deep sorrow and saying, 'Oh, for the fire of hell'"; Mu‘āwiyah wept on hearing this.

Before ‘Alī's death, Mu‘āwiyah met ‘Uday Ibn Ḥātam and intended to provoke him against ‘Alī (A.S.) so he asked him about his three sons who had been killed fighting for ‘Alī(A.S.). He wished to hear ‘Uday blame ‘Alī(A.S.) and so he said, "Was it fair of him to deprive you of your three sons and save his own sons from death in the battlefield?"

‘Uday answered, "It was I who was unfair to him. I should not be alive while he is buried in the earth." When Mu‘āwiyah saw that he had failed in his purpose, he asked ‘Uday to describe ‘Alī (A.S.)

fully for him, which he did. When he ended his narration, he noticed tears flowing down Mu'āwiyah's beard and wiping them with his sleeve, saying, "Alas! Time is too sterile to produce a man like 'Alī." You see how truth reveals itself.

But was Imām 'Alī only a pious man of the altar? No. We see him also as the most social being, well aware of the conditions of the poor and helpless and all who brought their complaints to him. Though he was a Caliph, he went among the people, dealing with their affairs. When he met merchants he shouted, "You should first go and learn Islamic questions of trade."[1] In other words, before engaging in commerce, they should know divine injunctions about what is lawful and unlawful in every deal. He is also reported to have used a phrase to a poor beggar who begged him for something. 'Alī (A.S.) looked at him and saw that he was capable of working but had chosen begging as a trade. He gave him advice and said, 'Follow your honor and dignity,' a phrase that he addressed to every person. For work brings dignity and honor.

'Alī (A.S.) is thus a true Muslim: Pious in worship, a just judge in the court, a brave soldier and commander on the battlefield, a fine orator at the pulpit, a remarkable teacher in his chair, and a wonderful and perfect example in every other accomplishment.

Islam can never approve of half-hearted acceptance of its injunctions or belief in some of them and not in others. This is a wrong way adopted by some ascetics who considered Islam to consist of praying, or those who ignored acts of devotion altogether.

---

1. Al-Ḥurr al-'Āmilī, *Wasā'il al-Shī'ah*, vol. 17, 381.

Portrait of a Muslim Community

The Qur'an says:

> Muḥammad is the Prophet (S) of God and those who are with him are hard against the unbelievers, compassionate among themselves. (48:29)

In this sentence, the feature of an Islamic community is portrayed. In the first part of it, the matter of following faith and the Prophet (S) is expressed and in the latter part, the question of standing firmly against infidels is mentioned. Thus these seeming devotees who make a mosque their home and say no word when they are driven on by a single soldier, are not Muslims. The most important quality of a Muslim according to the Qur'an is showing firmness and strength against an enemy.

The Qur'an says, 'Faint not, neither sorrow; you shall be the upper ones if you are believers.' (3:133) Islam does not allow weakness in religion. Will Durant says in his History of Civilization that no religion but Islam calls upon its followers to be so strong and steadfast.

To bend the neck with helplessness, to dress poorly and in a dirty way, to walk lazily and to pretend to be forelorn and indifferent to all around you and sigh and groan are all contrary to Islam. The Qur'an says, 'And as for the favor of your Lord, announce (it).' (93:11) God has given you blessings like health and strength. Why do you show yourself so helpless? This is ingratitude. 'Alī (A.S.) was never such a man. He stood ably and strongly against enemies.

What about being kind to others ? We sometimes meet devotees who are never kind and are usually glum and unsociable. They never laugh and seldom smile as if the whole of humanity is indebted to them and yet they suppose themselves to be attached to Islam. Is it enough to stand firmly against enemies and be kind to Muslims? The answer is no. The Qur'an says, 'You will see them bowing down, prostrating themselves, seeking grace from God and good pleasure.'(48:29) This speaks of those who have the two above qualities of steadfastness and kindness and in their prayers and prostrations sink so deeply in their devotion that you can see in their faces all signs of chastity and godliness.

It is narrated from the Prophet (S) that the disciples of Christ asked him with whom they should associate and he answered, "Sit with someone whose sight reminds you of God, whose speech increases your knowledge and whose conduct persuades you into doing good."[1] The verse continues, 'That is their description in the Old Testament and their description in the New Testament like a seed-produce that puts forth its sprout, then strengthens it so it becomes stout and stands firmly on its stem, delighting the sowers that He may enrage the unbelievers on account of them.' (48:29)

A nation possessing all the above attributes must be a remarkably find nation. Now, tell me, why should Muslims be so decadent, docile and miserable. Which of those qualities mentioned before do we possess? What should we expect? Although we admit that Islam is a social creed, why should we scorn worship and prayer and communion with God?

Heedlessness of the Prayers

Let me assure you that taking prayers lightly is a sin as ignoring them is a sin.

---

1. Muḥammad Ibn Ya'qūb Kulaynī, *Uṣūl min al-Kāfī*, vol. 1, 39.

On the death of Imām Ja'far Ṣādiq (A.S.) Abū Baṣrī came to offer Umm-e Ḥamīda his condolences, the latter wept and so did the former. Umm-e Ḥamīda then narrated something that had happened in the last moments of the life of the Imām. She said that he sank into a trance and then opened his eyes and asked for all his relatives to be present. After they had all gathered there, the Imām addressed them the following remark and then died. He said, "Those who take ritual prayers lightly will never gain our intercession."[1] You see that he did not speak of those who ignore ritual prayers altogether, for, the consequence of that is obvious. What does 'taking the ritual prayers lightly' mean? It means that in spite of having time, an opportunity, one may postpone them and just before it is getting too late, perform the acts of devotion hastily and perfunctorily, without giving the mind and spirit the necessary tranquility before beginning to say the ritual prayer.

Experience has shown that in a household where ritual prayers are taken lightly, no interest is shown by its members to pray or to pray properly. One should choose a spot in the house allotted to acts of devotion, or, if possible, a separate room for them and carry on with ablution without haste and spread a clean prayer-carpet and accompany all the preliminary acts with the convocation of God.

Imām 'Alī's Ablution

'Alī (A.S.) began with, "In the Name of God and with the help of God. Oh God place me among those who repent; place me among those who cleanse themselves."[2]

1. Al-Ḥurr al-'Āmilī, *Wasā'il al-Shī'ah*, vol. 4,25.
2. *Ibid*, vol. 1, 401.

Two nights ago I spoke about repentance and explained that repentance meant purifying oneself. Washing the body is the prelude to purifying the spirit; it refreshens the face, but since the intention is to cleanse the spirit, too, it gives one a sacred aspect. 'Alī (A.S.) in his ablution prayed to God to illuminate his face on the Day of the Resurrection where many faces are black with shame and sin. Then he said this prayer on washing his right hand, "Oh God, on the Day of Resurrection, put my book of deeds in my right hand,"[1] and on washing his left hand, he said, "Oh God, do not give me my book of deeds in my left hand nor from behind my back. Oh God, do not let it be shackled to my neck; I seek refuge from You from the fire of hell."

Then, on touching his forehead with water, he said, "Merge me into your grace and blessings." Then on touching his feet with water he said, "Oh God, direct my efforts towards such a path of your satisfaction."[2]

Such an ablution which is accompanied by so many pleadings is of a different worth and merit than what most of us are accustomed to perform. We should not lightly disregard all these rites and confine ourselves only to the absolutely obligatory parts.

Let us see what religious authorities say about this. Should we repeat the following sentence three times or only once, "Glory be to God, praise be God, there is no god but God and God is great." An authority may say, "Once is enough, since it is obligatory but the second and third repetitions are recommended." Should we, on the basis of this verdict, confine ourselves to saying this prayer only once?

1. Ibid.
2. Ibid.

Heedlessness of Other Acts of Worship

In the same way, fasting may be taken lightly. I am saying this as a joke, but if I were God I would not accept such fasts. I know some people who stay awake at night in the month of Ramadhan, not to worship and pray, but to drink tea, smoke and eat fruit. In the morning, they say their ritual prayers and go to sleep. Some of them sleep all day and wake up near sunset to say their daily ritual prayers hastily before it is too late and get ready to break their fast. What kind of a fast is this? When you do not give yourself the chance of feeling the pain of abstemiousness? This is fasting lightly and is really an insult to a fast.

Again we go on a pilgrimage to Mecca but perform the rites lightly in the same way as our prayers and fasts. Similarly the matter of the call to prayer may be taken lightly; it is said that the call to prayer should be utterest melodiously to attract and invite people to prayer, in the same way that the Qur'an should be recited clearly, fluently and with a fine voice. Some people are gifted with a fine voice, but if you ask them to sing out the call to prayer, they consider it below their dignity to be known as a mū'adhdhin. But it is really an honor to be one. Imām 'Alī(A.S.) himself was one, even when he was a Caliph. There is no disgrace attached to this task and no nobility to forsake it.

Thus no act of worship should be taken lightly. The merit of Islam is in its comprehensiveness, not in being so absorbed in devotion as to ignore every other duty, nor to be so involved in social matters to forget acts of devotion. Although a prayer is for its own sake and for proximity to God, if we scorn worship, we are ignoring other duties, too. Worship is the executive and guarantor of other Islamic injunctions.

Here I end my discourse and pray God to make us true worshippers, to acquaint us with the comprehensiveness of Islam, to make us whole-hearted Muslims, grant us pure intentions, forgive our sins in these precious nights, and grant salvation to our deceased ones.

Discourse 7
Worship and Prayer II

> Surely prayer keeps (one) away from indecency and dishonor and certainly the remembrance of God is the greatest. (29:44)

In Islam, acts of devotion, in addition to their preeminence, are a part of its educational program. By genuineness is meant being a goal of creation irrespective of the matter of human life in any other respect. The Qur'an says, 'And I have not created jinn and mankind except to worship Me.' (51:59)

Worship is a means of the human being's proximity to God as well as one's true perfection. That is, that which is the manifestation of the human being's perfection is, at the same time, a goal in itself. It desires to train individuals morally and socially and so a means has been adopted which is most effective on human morals and spirit. It enables one to forget the self and self-interests.

Faith as the Supporter of Morality and Justice

In social matters, the basic principle is justice, which is respecting other people's rights. This is the main difficulty of humanity in both morality and society. There is no one who is ignorant of morality and its necessity. The difficulty is practising it. When a human being wants to put this principle into practice, that person is faced with interests on one side and morality on the other; truthfulness on one side and profit on the other. One should either resort to falsehood and treason in order to gain profit, or tell the truth and forsake profit. Here we see a man who speaks of justice, acting against ethics and justice in practice. The only thing that acts as a support to the human being's morality and justice and enables one to forsake profit is faith. Faith in what? In justice and morality themselves. When a person believes in both justice and morality as something sacred? When a person has faith in the basis of sacredness, namely God. So, a person is bound to both justice and morality to the same extent that one is bound to God, and has faith in Him.

This is the problem of our time: That science is supposed to be sufficient for mankind. If we recognize justice and morality and act according to them, we can be both just and moral. But it is actually shown that when knowledge is separate from faith, not only is it not useful for morality and justice, it is harmful. As Sanā'ī, the poet, says, "When a thief carries a light, he can pick more choice objects." But with faith, both morality and justice will endure. In Islam, worship of God is not set up as something separate from morality and justice.

To illustrate this point, here is a question. Where in the world have you seen a guilty person come forth voluntarily for punishment? A guilty person usually flees from justice. The only force that can make a human being voluntarily submit to punishment is faith. We see many examples of this in early Islam. Islam has envisaged punishment for all sins, such as drinking, adultery and theft. At the same time it says, "Punishments are abandoned with the slightest doubt." Islam does not compel a judge or governor to seek out a guilty person; rather it places an urge within a guilty person to come forward for punishment. This kind of thing often happened in the time of both the Prophet (S)and Imām ʻAlī. A man would come before them begging to be punished in order to purify himself.

A man came to the Prophet, confessing adultery. In such matters the confession should be repeated four times to be credible. The Prophet (S)said, "*Maybe you mean you kissed her*?" The man said, "No. It was adultery." The Prophet (S)said again, "*Perhaps you only gave her a pinch,* " hoping again that he would say ,"Yes," and he would then be pardoned. But the man gave a negative answer. This dialogue went on until it was quite clear that adultery had been committed and the man begged for punishment in order to be relieved of punishment in the next world.

There is another case of a woman who came to ʻAlī (A.S.) and said, "Oh Commander of the Faithful, I am married and in the absence of my husband, I have committed adultery and I am now pregnant. I wish to be purified from my sin." Imām ʻAlī said, "One confession is not sufficient. It should be repeated four times." Then he said, "The punishment for the adultery of a married woman is being stoned to death. If you are dealt this punishment, what happens to the baby in your womb? The baby has done no wrong and must not be stoned. Go away until your baby is born."

After a few months, the woman came again. This time with a baby in her arms and asked to be purified since the baby was born . This was her second confession. Again ʻAlī (A.S.) said, "We might stone you but this baby is not guilty. It needs milk and a mother to nurse it. So, go away now since the baby needs you."

The woman returned home uneasily and after two years reappeared before the Imām , and said, "Purify me now as the baby has been weaned and is growing up." ʻAlī (A.S.) said, "Go away. This child still needs a mother." The mother wept and said, "Oh God, I have confessed three times but the Imām has sent me away three times and refused to stone me. I cannot bear being polluted with sin."

As it happened, a hypocrite called ʻAmr Ibn Ḥarīz saw the woman and asked what the matter was. She explained what had happened and the man said, "I will settle this. Give me the child and let me be his guardian."[1] She was not aware that ʻAlī wanted her not to make the fourth confession.

They went back to ʻAlī (A.S.) and the woman asked to be purified since the man had agreed to look after the child and insisted on receiving the punishment. ʻAlī (A.S.) felt very uncomfortable that the matter reached a point where no alternative was left for him but to order her to be punished.

This is an example of true faith in religion capturing one's conscience and making one submit to justice. The purpose of worship is to revive one's religious life and give it freshness and strength. The greater one's faith, the more one turns to God and the less one sins. Sinning and not sinning are not the concern of knowledge; they are the concern of faith and neglecting faith leads to sinfulness.

The Meaning of Innocence

Let me explain a point about the immaculateness of Prophets and Imāms. What does this mean? You may say they never sin.

---

1. Muḥammad Bāqir Majlisī, *Biḥār al-Anwār*, vol. 76, 45-48.

That is true, but there are two answers to this. One is that God intentionally prevents them from sinning. If this is the case, then sinlessness is not an accomplishment. If this is the case, no one could sin, since he is hindered by a power beyond himself. Therefore Prophets and Imāms may be supposed to have no superiority over other people except that they are treated discriminately by God. So it is not a question of their desiring to sin but being prevented from doing so by God.

Purity is a high degree of faith in God and thinking constantly of him. A person without faith rarely or never thinks of God; that person is altogether negligent. There are others who are occasionally negligent and commit sins in this state of negligence, but when they turn to God, they naturally avoid sin. But if faith attains a perfect state of permanently thinking of God, a person is never negligent and every act of that person is based on faith.

The Qur'an refers to 'those who are engaged in trade but never forget God.' (34:37) It does not speak of avoiding trade and commerce. Islam does not prohibit trading. On the contrary it encourages work and commerce and at the same time expects one to think of God and therefore never sin.

Let me give an example. Has it ever happened to you to put your hand in the fire knowingly-? It does not as a rule happen unless you wish to burn yourself. Why do we avoid fire? Because our knowledge tells us it is dangerous and we are sure of this knowledge. In this way we are pure in relation to fire and our certainty and belief about fire serves as a check.

The friends of God, too, are innocent since they are certain of the burning power of sins and thus, thinking of God and thereby being attached to morality, justice and rights, enables them to avoid sin. In Islam the life of both worlds is inter-related. Christianity, on the other hand, separates the reckoning of each world.

The Prayers Being in Company with Other Affairs:

1. Social Rights and Purity

For example the other-worldly aspect of the Islamic prayer is thinking of God and fearing Him, otherwise why should so many rites be necessary. Being clean in body makes no difference to God for proximity to Him for He says, ‘When you stand up for the prayer you should have first performed ablution by washing your face and hands as far as the elbows.’

Cleanliness has been combined with acts of devotion. Again according to the injunction, "When your body is unclean, you must wash yourself completely." Your place of worship must be lawful and not usurped. So must be your prayer-carpet and your clothes. If one single thread of these is gained illegitimately, your prayer is null and void. Again, worship must be combined with respect for others' rights. If a house is seized by force, praying in it is invalid for him who has violated the owner's right. Such a house should have either been bought by the latter in order to render his acts of worship correct, or the owner's satisfaction should have been secured first. The same applies to clothes and carpets. Moreover if a religious tax is due on the property of the worshipper, it should have been paid.

2. Knowledge of *Qibla*

Then we are told to face the Ka‘ba in the prayer. Where is the Ka‘ba? It is the first temple built in the world for the worship of God. Everyone should perform the ritual prayer standing facing the direction of the first mosque built by the Prophets Abraham and Ismāʿīl. Why should we face it? Is God there? The Qur'an says, 'Whither so ever you turn, there is the Face of God.' Why should we face the Kaʿba? It is meant as a social education for all to face one spot, for, facing any direction one wants, means dispersion and confusion. Thus facing the first temple is devotion.

3. Punctuality

Again we are told that there is a definite time for devotion, even to the minute. Morning ritual prayer times is between dawn and sunrise, and performing it even a minute before dawn or a minute after sunrise makes it void. You cannot offer the excuse of being sleepy, for, this has no meaning for God since all hours are the same to Him. But the purpose of regarding time is to train and educate human beings. The same punctuality applies also to noon, afternoon, evening and night prayers. Prayer and worship are inseparable.

4. Emotion Controlling

In praying you are not free to do what you like, such as crying in memory of something unpleasant or laughing at a funny incident. Praying is the control of feelings. There is no turning to any side but the point in front, no glancing at anything which might attract your attention. Nor are you allowed to eat or drink while praying. All such diversions are contrary to the spirit of worship, which requires total self-control.

5. Gravity

Another point is bodily control. Unnecessary movements of the limbs in standing position, in bowing and prostration are not allowed. The whole body must be calm and stable before the phrase *allāhu akbar* is uttered. If you feel pain in some part of your body, rest awhile in the same position before resuming your prayer.

6. Peace-Making with all Virtuous People

Now we come to other parts of the prayer which means attention to God only, and we utter the phrase, "Greetings to all worthy servants of God." This is a declaration of peace and goodwill towards all good beings. This means mingling worship of God with educational matters. In spiritual matters, the more one forgets one's self, the better it is, but from a social viewpoint, one should never forget others.

In the first chapter of the Holy Qur'an which we recite as part of the ritual prayer, 'We worship only You, Oh, God, and beg only Your help.' Here we do not use the word 'I' but 'we' to show that all Muslims are inter-related in an Islamic community. In Islam, 'I' is always replaced by 'we'. All these are lessons to learn. When we *say allāhu akbar* are we expressing our fear of God? It is natural for the human being to be afraid of anything which is great, whether it is a mountain, a sea, or a powerful person. But when we say "God is Greater," in a convinced manner, nothing else and no one can frighten us by their greatness, for God is Greater than anything we may imagine and all other things are trivial in comparison with Him.

Imām ʻAlī says, "God has manifested Himself in the spirit of the true believers and thus everything else unrelated to God seems small in their eyes."[1]

Smallness and greatness are, of course, relative. If you were in a smaller place before coming here, this hall would seem very large to you; the reverse is also true. Therefore, those who are acquainted with the greatness of God, consider other things insignificant. Saʻdī says that for mystics nothing exists but God and only those who understand truth realize the

---

1. Imām ʻAlī, *Nahj al-Balāghah*, 303.

meaning of his words, while others criticize him lor those words. He then asks, "If there exists nothing but God then what are the heaven and earth and men and monsters and beasts?" He answers this question himself by saying that all these things are too small to say they exist as compared with God's existence. He then compares this with an ocean and a drop of water and with the sun and a tiny particle.

The Influence of the Phrase "God Is the Greatest"

When you utter the phrase "God is Greater" in all sincerity, His greatness is personified before you and thus nothing else finds enough significance to be flattered or feared or shown humbleness. In this way, devotion to God brings freedom: you become God's servant but free in relation to everything else. Each of the following words in the ritual prayer has a meaning illustrating God's greatness: "God is great. Glory be to God. Praise belongs to God. Glory be to my great Lord and I am praising Him. Glory be to my great Lord and I am praising Him. Glory be to my Lord the Most High and I am praising Him."

Many other phrases have been used in the ritual prayers. Someone asked 'Alī (A.S.) why in each cycle of the ritual prayer there are two prostrations and only one bowing. You know, of course, that prostration shows more humility than bowing. In prostrating, the head, which is the dearest part of the body, is placed on the low earth, as a sign of humility and worship.

In answer, 'Alī (A.S.) said, "In the first prostration you are reminding yourself that you are made of dust and in the second one you remember that you will die and return to dust and by raising your head once more, you will think of the day you will be raised again for a future life."

Our Responsibility of Encouraging Our Families to Perform Prayers

Let me tell you in connection with the importance of daily prayers that each of us is responsible, not only for the performance of one's own acts of devotion, but also for that of the other members of one's household. This phrase is addressed to the Prophet: "Bid your family to pray and be patient in it." This Command is not only for the Prophet; all of us are duty- bound to it.

What about children? Should they be trained to perform ritual prayer from childhood? The injunction is that children should be taught to perform the ritual prayers from the age of seven. They cannot, of course, yet utter the sentences with the correct pronunciation but they can be trained to observe the form of it as a habit when they begin their elementary education. It should, however, be remembered that force must not be used in this matter. They should be encouraged and give the chance to perform it willingly. There are many ways of encouragement such as praising, rewarding, showing greater affection and providing an environment conducive to such a performance.

Taking a child to congregational ritual prayer in a mosque is an effective way of encouragement and religious training. Even adults are greatly influenced by the spirit of worship in a group. Negligence in making habitual visits to places of devotion causes a frequent lack of inclination towards ritual prayer. This is especially true of children who have not been brought up to regard this as a religious duty and who when they reach the age of manhood, they are quite indifferent towards it.

If the objection is raised that mosques are often not kept clean enough to attract people or that preacher's sermons are sometimes boring, these are matters which could be remedied and not a reason to ignore a religious duty. The Qur'an says, 'What brought you into hell? They shall answer, 'We were not of those who prayed, neither did we feed the poor and we used to talk vanities with vain talkers.' (74:43-46)

Now you understand why in Islam the ritual prayer has been called a pillar of religion by the Prophet, for everything will be accepted when the ritual prayer is correctly performed. In his last moment of life, 'Alī (A.S.) invited people to take the remark of the Prophet (S) about prayer most seriously.[1]

Imām Ḥusain's Prayers in Karbala Desert

You may have heard that on 'Āshūrā (the 10th of Muḥarram when Imām Ḥusain and his followers were martyred), the martyrdom of Imām Ḥusain took place in the afternoon, so by noon most of the Imām 's household and companions were still alive, and only thirty of them were killed before noon. One of the Imām 's companions realized suddenly that it was noon and the time to perform the ritual prayer. He begged the Imām for a collective prayer for the last time. The Imām agreed and said, "You have remembered your ritual prayer so may God make you a devoted man in praying."

It was fitting for this warrior to be spoken of thus by the Imām. At any rate, they performed the ritual prayer together on the battlefield, a ritual prayer which is called 'ritual prayer of fear' in jurisprudence, consisting of two cycles instead of four since it must be brief enough to see the line of defence against the enemy

1. Ibid, 421.

when half of the army prays and the other half is on the alert in case of enemy attack. Then the groups change places for performing the ritual prayer and military duty.

Imām Ḥusain(A.S.)performed the ritual paryer in this manner, not far from the enemy's line. The shameless enemy did not even at this moment leave them at peace and continued their assaults with their bows and arrows and by their biting tongues, sneering at these devouted soldiers. Two of the men who shielded the Imām in his ritual prayer fell by the enemy's arrows. One of them was Sa'īd bin 'Abdullāh Ḥanafī who was at the point of death when the Imām finished his ritual prayer. When the Imām went to him, Sa'īd said, "Oh Abū 'Abdillāh. Have I done my duty? Implying that he would have wished to do more."

This was Imām Ḥusain's ritual prayer in Karbalā. In the battlefield of Karbalā, he was bowing forward when he received an arrow in his chest, which he draws out from his back. In his prostration, when the right side of his face was on the earth, for he could not lay his forehead on the ground as he had fallen off his horse. At this moment, he said, "In the Name of God and with the help of God and with the religion of the Prophet (S) of God and there is neither might nor power but in God the Most High, the Great. Oh God bless Muhammad and his chaste family."

In conclusion I pray God grant us a happy end, give us the favor of worship and devotion to Him, make us true performers of ritual prayer make our intentions pure, protect us against jinn and human beings, and grant salvation to our deceased ones.

Discourse 8
Repentance I

> And (remember) Jonah when he went forth enraged and thought that We would have no power over him, then he called out, "There is no God but You. Glory be to You. I have done evil." So We answered him and delivered him out of grief even so do We deliver the believers. (21:87-8)

In my last two discourses, I explained that worship and prayer, if correctly performed, eventually leads to a true affinity to God. The human being, through worship, will be a real servant of God and a real servant has a true affinity to God. In other words, to be a real servant of God implies a sacred journey which culminates in affinity to God.

Tonight I wish to discuss the first stage of the sacred journey, the point where we must begin our journey towards affinity to God. And this is what we need today. We, who have not taken any steps in this sacred path, will not benefit from discussing the higher stages of those travelling this path.

If we are practical beings, we should realize the first step and the first stage and how we should begin our worship.

The first step on the path of affinity to God is repentance, which is the topic of my talk tonight.

Analysis of Repentance from a Psychological Viewpoint

What does repentance means and what is its nature psychologically and what is its consequence spiritually? For many of us, it seems a simple matter but have we ever thought of analyzing it psychologically? Repentance is a characteristic of the human being that sets it apart from animals. The human being possesses certain high aptitudes and distinctive qualities which are not found in animals. One of these is the ability to repent. It does not mean only uttering the phrase, "I seek forgiveness from God, the Most High and I repent to Him."

It is not something verbal. It is a psychological and spiritual state, a revolution of the mind and the above phrase describes that state but it is not the state itself. So if we utter this phrase several times a day, it does not mean we are penitent. True repentance once a day brings us stage by stage nearer to God.

As an introduction, let me say that there is a difference between inanimate and living things in the fact that inanimate things have not the ability to change the course they follow by their own power such as the revolution of the earth around the sun or the movement of the stars in their orbits or a stone which is dropped from a height and pulled down by the force of gravity. There must be an external factor to be able to deliver them from their habitual course.

On the other hand, living things such as plants and animals have the ability to change their course from within themselves and if they meet conditions which do not accord with their life and its continuation, they themselves change their course. When a sheep, a pigeon or even a fly meets an obstacle in its way, it will change its course even to the extent of a hundred and eighty degrees, thus moving in quite the opposite direction.

Even plants can choose and change their course within certain limits and conditions. When the roots of a tree reach a stone, they change its course.

The human being, too, is similar to plants and animals in this matter. Repentance is in fact a change of the course, not a simple one like that of plants and animals, rather something much more complex and worthy of analysis.

Repentance is an internal revolution of the human being against the self. Plants and animals do not act against themselves yet the human being has the ability to do so. The rise of one group of human beings against another group is a natural and obvious matter since we expect the oppressed to arise against the oppressor. This is also true of the rise of one country or nation against another country or nation. But the rise of a person against the self is not so simple and obvious. Why does it happen?

Man, a Complex Person

The reason is that, in spite of having one body, a human being is intellectually and spiritually a complex being. The human being is a mixture of animal ferocity and passion, on the one hand, and of angelic qualities on the other. Sometimes the pig takes over the command as a lustful being, giving no choice to the ferocious beast, devil or angel within to act. Suddenly one part rebels against this rule and subverts it in favor of the domination of another of its aspects.

A sinful being is one who is dominated by the beast or devil within by which the angel and its noble qualities are imprisoned. Repentance is the arising of the noble qualities within against one's own mean and wicked aspects, putting an end to their domination and destroying all their force.

The converse is also true and the base aspects of the human being can defeat the noble aspects and govern the person to its own destruction. It is true that all the instincts and forces granted to human beings have some use and must be employed in their proper place and time. But there is a limit for each of them which must be observed.

A horse and dog must be taken care of in order to be useful. There are conditions for proper attention to them and a limit to using them. For a child, play is a necessity for the excess of energy to be spent and for the child to learn. It would be miss-education to hinder the child from its natural playfulness. It would be unnatural to force it to attend the society of adults. It would be wrong of a clergyman to compel his young son to wear the garment and turban of a mullah and to prevent him from following his natural desire of playing with other children.

You may have come across children who, at their father's persistent suggestion, engage in ritual prayer and other acts of devotion for many years but when they attain manhood they are suddenly changed into libertines who know no limit in their debauchery. Why is it so? Because natural instincts have long been suppressed on the excuse of promoting higher spiritual education. Of course, inclination towards godliness and worship forms a part of a child's nature but these should not be strengthened at the price of checking all his other natural instincts, each of which has a share and importance in developing a perfect human being. Otherwise, when by chance a child sees a sexy film or meets a woman, the whole of the structure which has been forcefully imposed upon him will collapse causing irreparable damage and ruin.

Repentance is quite the reverse of the above conduct. When a person sinks deeply into sin and lust, and the angel within is not satiated, a catastrophe suddenly occurs. A human being does not have only one mouth; it has hundreds of mouths to be fed, the mouth of desire, the mouth of love, and the mouth of worship. The spirit must be fed with worship and devotion. But when it is starved, the subsequent uneasiness is terrible. A young man who is well off and for whom everything has been provided, suddenly commits suicide. Everyone wonders why he did so. The reason is that a holy power had been imprisoned in him causing him so much pain that it was beyond his endurance and he chose that way out. You meet someone living a luxurious life in a lovely garden and yet he is dissatisfied and uncomfortable. For he lacks the spiritual pleasures which he needs and which must be produced from within him, not from the outside.

Thus, repentance is a reaction of the holy, and noble spirit of the human being against the lower animal self; a holy rebellion of the angelic side against the evil and beastly vices within.

How does this retrocession occur?

Conditions of Appearance of Repentance

You should firstly remember that if the holy elements in the human being's personality go wholly out of action and are so completely fettered as to make release impossible, then one cannot gain the divine favor of repentance. But just as the presence of only a few virtuous and chaste people in a country may motivate a revolution, so the existence of a few fine and noble elements in a human being will make repentance possible. If one knows God, this repentance may take the form of turning to God. If not, it will take some other form and may even lead to madness.

We called repentance a reaction. When you throw a ball down, it rebounds. Throwing it is an action and the rebound is its reaction. How high the ball rebounds depends on two things: Firstly, the intensity of the action, namely the sin. If it is small, the reaction will be small and if it is great, the reaction in the spirit will be great. So the more cruel a person is, and the bigger his crime, the more intense will be the reaction. The American pilot of the plane which bombed Hiroshima, on looking down at the city he had bombed and the old and young people he had destroyed, felt such a pang of conscience that when he returned to his country to receive his countrymen's welcome and the wreath around his neck, he was a changed man altogether, even though he had been picked for that task in the first place for his cruelty and indifference. He may have smiled at the words of praise showered on him but in the privacy of his home when he was alone with his conscience he felt such a criminal that he ended his life in a lunatic asylum.

Busr Ibn Arṭāt was a most cruel general of Mu'āwiyah. A policy of Mu'āwiyah was to send him or other equally hard-hearted men at the head of an army to penetrate the frontiers of 'Alī's realm and do as much damage as possible; They were given a free hand to kill, burn, pillage and destroy. This Busr once attacked Yemen, committing many crimes including the capture and beheading of the two small sons of 'Ubaidullāh Ibn 'Abbās, 'Alī's cousin, who was the governor there. Later his conscience troubled him so much for this ugly deed that neither in his sleep nor while awake even for a moment could he forget this bloody action. Finally he went out and rode a wooden horse in the street with a wooden sword in one hand and a whip in the other, followed by groups of children hooting and laughing at him.

The second factor on which the intensity of the reaction of repentance depends is the nature of a person's conscience and the strength of his faith. That is why even small blunders which may hardly be called sins rouse the conscience of those who are spiritually firm and strong, while most of us may commit hundreds of these blunders every day without worrying about them.

Remembering the Late Ḥājj Mīrzā ʻAlī Āqā Shīrāzī

Chaste and spiritually strong people are constantly in a state of penitence. One such man was my great teacher, the late Ḥāj Mīrzā ʻAlī Āqā Shīrāzī. Once he visited us at Qum and then invited me to accompany him to a gathering, where, as it happened, the choicest pieces of both Persian and Arabic poetry were recited . He took an active part in the discussions and was amongst those who recited some poetry. Never did I realize that he had such a profound knowledge in this field. The poetry was of the poets Saʻdī and Ḥāfiẓ and others like them. Of course, to recite poems, especially poems like this, is no sin. But to recite poems at night is undesirable and when we left that house he kept on repeating words of repentance as if he had committed a great sin while many of us would not have worried about acts which may have been considered even more wrong.

The punishment that God has appointed for such beings is such that we are not worthy of them. This man was in the habit of rising two hours before dawn and it was by his example that I understood the meaning of devotion, godliness, penitence and complete absorption in God. But the next morning he happened to wake up later than his habitual hour for prayer and he declared that this was God's punishment for his listening to poetry the night before. In this man's belief, a man who wastes two hours at such an occupation is not worthy of two hours of necessary convocation with God.

I can cite you another example. If you leave a clear mirror in a place where you think, the air is pure and fine, you will see a layer of dust collected on it an hour later even though you had not felt that any dust was in the air before or on the wall or furniture. When a wall is dirty no stain shows on it in an obvious way and if it is blackened with tar, you cannot distinguish any trace of dirt or stain on it.

When the Prophet (S) sat in a gathering, he uttered the following words of penitence many times: I feel traces of turbidity on my heart and every day I repent for them seventy times."[1] Such things seem like a clear mirror to us while for him they are dimness and turbidity. Even talking to us human beings about God may seem turbidity to him in spite of seeing God in the mirror of our existence.

It has been narrated by Umm-e Salamah and others that for two months before his death, wherever the Prophet (S) sat or did something, he always uttered the following prayer, "Glory be to God. I seek forgiveness from Him and I repent to Him." She says, "I asked him why he uttered words of repentance so often and he answered that he was commanded to do so. It was later that we realized that the last chapter of the Qur'an had been revealed to him and he felt that it was a declaration of his

---

1. Ḥusain Nūrī al-Tabrisī, *Mustadrak al-Wasā'il wa Mustanbaṭ al-Masā'il*, vol. 5. 320.

end." This was sūra 110, having those three verses, 'When comes the help of God and victory and you see men entering God's religion in throngs, then proclaim the praise of your Lord and seek His forgiveness for He is the Acceptor of Forgiveness.'

This chapter was revealed to him even later than the verses concerning the completion of religion of Islam and the succession of 'Alī (A.S.) and it informed him that his task was done and it was time for the Prophet (S)to think of himself and this is why he continually glorified God and sought His forgiveness.

But we poor creatures are like that tarred wall and repeated sins produce no reaction in our spirit. I do not know where and for how long in our spirit we have been imprisoned that we see no signs of regret for our dark past and realize that we had gone astray and must now turn to God. Then we will be at the starting point of our heavenly journey.

Imām 'Alī's Advice

A man came to 'Alī (A.S.) asking for advice. He said, "Be not one of those who long for the next life but do nothing for it."[1] This is actually what some of us are like. We claim to love 'Alī (A.S.) but it is not real love for if it were, we would accompany it with action. Such people suppose that 'Alī (A.S.) needs a crowd, even if they are not true followers. The same behavior is true of those who weep for Imām Ḥusain (A.S.) unaccompanied by good deeds. But if it were true love, they would do something to prove it.

The second advice of 'Alī (A.S.) was, "Be not one of those who feel repentance to be necessary and yet they postpone it." People often think that they are too young to start repenting

1. Imām 'Alī, *Nahj al-Balāghah*, 497.

for they see old people engaged in worship and penitence. But the truth is that the time for repentance is youth. A young branch can be straightened, but when it grows thicker it does not lend itself to a change of shape. In old age no strength is left to make penitence practicable. By that time, our back is too bent with sin to make repentance effective. Rūmī, the poet, tells a story about a man who had planted a bramble on the people's path. When it grew up, he was asked to uproot it but he said, "It is too early, there is no hurry. It is easily uprooted." He kept on offering the same excuse year after year. But the brambles grew thicker and its roots firmer and its thorns sharper and more dangerous, while the man grew older and weaker and unable to pull it out by the root.

The poet means that vices take root rapidly in a person. You can remove them when you are young but as you grow older, you become more and more helpless against them. It is then too late to do anything. I swear by God that even one hour's delay is important; so is one night and one day. Today is better for repentance than tomorrow and tonight better than tomorrow night. Worship is no use without repentance. Just as one washes oneself for ritual prayer, so one should first repent before one performs an act of devotion whether it is praying, fasting, reading the Qur'an, going on a pilgrimage or even attending sermons.

Someone came to 'Alī (A.S.) claiming strongly his intention to repent. The Imām realized that he was not serious and asked him, "Do you know what repentance is? It is an act worthy of exalted being; it is a holy state of mind which makes you feel that God has bestowed His grace on you and that you are surrounded by angels. You lose your egoism and feel you are purified." In repentance there is no need to go to a clergyman or to another human being. Repent to your God as it is said in the Qur'an, Says, 'Oh my people who have been prodigal against yourselves, do not despair of God's Mercy," surely God forgives sins altogether.' (39:53)

A Sacred Tradition

The following sentence has been quoted in a Sacred Tradition, The groan (of repentance) of sinners is dearer to Me than the glorified glorifications (of Me) so you should sigh and groan in these precious nights. Be your own judge and censor, confess all your sins and be sure that God will forgive you and purify your soul. Then you taste the sweetness of worship and sin and the pleasure obtained from them will seem to you so trifling that you will never feel inclined to commit them anymore nor to lie or slander or accuse others.

'Alī (A.S.) has considered six conditions necessary for repentance: Two form its basis, two are the requisites for its acceptance and two for its completion. These six points will be explained in my next discourse.

The greatest joy of chaste people has always been to admit to God their shortcomings, their faults, their needs and their poverty, saying that they show nothing but negligence, while God grants nothing but favor and grace. The following prayer is quoted from Imām 'Alī Ibn Ḥusain (A.S.),

> My Master, when I glance at my sins I am overcome by fear but when I glance at Your Grace I am filled with hope.[1]

Let me say a few words about the tragedy of Karbalā. On the 9th of Muḥarram, the day before the martyrdom of Imām Ḥusain

1. Shaykh 'Abbās Qummī, *Mafātiḥ al-Janān,* Du'ā-ye Abū Ḥamzah.

(A.S.)the army of 'Umar Ibn Sa'd launched their assault on the orders of 'Ubidullāh Ibn Ziyād intending to give battle at night. Imām Ḥusain(A.S.)asked through his brother, Abul Faḍl al-'Abbās for a respite of one night. To remove suspicion that he intended to delay the fight, he said, Dear brother, God Himself knows that I love to offer my ritual prayers to Him and tonight which is the last night of my life, I am more eager to do so and to offer my repentance and beg His Forgiveness.

It was a wonderful night of joy for them, full of hopes of martyrdom. They made themselves neat and tidy and even cut their hair. They set aside one of the tents especially for this. One person would be inside and two men were standing outside when one of them began joking. The other one told him that it was no occasion for mirth and joy. He answered that as a rule he did not joke but he felt that night to be a night for mirth.

When others (the enemy) approached the tents, they heard sounds like the buzzing of bees and asked what it was.[1] They were told that the Imām, his household and companions were busy praying and invoking God's Name. The Imām spent that night in devotion and worship. He saw to the affairs of his family and it was then that he delivered his last, eloquent sermon to his followers.

The Repentant Of Karbala Desert

Let me mention a penitent of Karbalā that night, a real penitent whose repentance was accepted: Ḥurr Ibn Yazīd Riyāḥī. He was a brave warrior of Kūfa. When Ibn Ziyād wanted to send a thousand men for the first time against Imām Ḥusain(A.S.)Ḥurr was the man chosen. In doing so he

---

1. Sayyid Ibn Ṭāwūs, *Luhūf alā Qatlā al-Ṭufūf*, 91.

oppressed and mistreated the Prophet's household. It is said that Ḥurr was seen to be trembling like a leaf. The same narrator was surprised and, approaching him, asked him the reason and whether he was afraid. Ḥurr told him,

> No. I have no fear of fighting but I see myself at a cross roads between heaven and hell and I am wondering which route to take.

At last he chose the right route. Slowly, slowly he turned his horse away in such a way that no one knew what he intended to do. When he reached a certain point, he spurred his horse on until he reached the Imām's tent with his shield turned backward as a sign of coming in peace.

On seeing the Imām, he cried out, "Is my repentance acceptable?"[1] Then the Imām said, "Yes." His chivalry was such that he did not put one word of blame upon him for his past conduct. Ḥurr begged the Imām to let him go and fight. The Imām said, "You are our guest. Get down off your horse and stay with us awhile." But he felt shy, whispering to himself with shame for his past, for having sinned against the family of the Prophet. That is why he again requested that Imām Ḥusain let him go and fight the attacking foes lest one of the children look at him and cause him to die of shame.

---

1. Ibid, 101.

Discourse 9
Repentance II

> Lord we have wronged ourselves and if You do not forgive us, and have mercy upon us, we shall surely be among the lost. (7:23)

In my previous discourse, I explained that repentance is the first step of the devotees on the journey of affinity to God and I promised to mention in this discourse the explanation of Imām 'Alī (A.S.)about the conditions and phases of repentance. Before doing so, I wish to answer this question, "When is the time for repentance and when is it accepted?"

Opportunity for Repentance

A person has the opportunity to repent as long as that person is alive and before death comes. When a person is in the cloches of death, no time is left to be saved through repentance. According to traditional interpretations, this death time is the moment that one feels and sees death and gets a glimpse of the next world.

Repentance in the next world has no meaning for one is not in a position to repent nor can it be real. But the reason why at the time of death repentance is not acceptable, is explained in the Qur'an.

> Then when they saw Our might, they said, 'We believe in God alone and we disbelieve in that we were associating with Him.' But their belief when they saw Our might did not profit them ... (40:84)

Why is it so? Because repentance does not mean simply regret or a return from the wrong path due to one factor or another. Repentance is real when an internal revolution takes place in a person, causing a rise against all lustful, evil forces and wicked deeds, and domination over them all.

Seeing divine vengeance approaching and then experiencing belief and repenting is not an internal revolution. The Qur'an says about Pharaoh:

> Till when the drowning overtook him, he said, ' I believe that there is no god but He in whom the Children of Israel believe.'(10:90)

As long as Pharaoh alive he acts like a despot and nothing and no counsel convinced him. He resorts to a contest between his magicians and Moses; he shows more rebelliousness and decides to kill Moses and his tribe. He chases them in their flight and, when he is at the point of drowning in the sea and there is no escape, he repents and expresses his belief in the God of Moses. But it is too late for his repentance to be acceptable for it is not a real, internal revolution. His repentance is only due to his helplessness in a calamity. So they say to him, "Now? When you previously rebelled?" In other words, "Why did you not repent an hour before when you were quite free to do so?" For, then, it would have been a true change of heart. What criminal in the world is not penitent at the moment of punishment? But if he shows a regret and penitence before he is caught, then we can say he is changing spiritually.

Now, as for why repentance in the next world is unacceptable, this is because the criminal witnesses punishment there and the consequence of his deeds and therefore his repentance would not be a true revolution. Moreover, death is like the fall of a fruit from the tree. As long as it is a part of the tree, it is dependent on the air, water and nourishment that the tree obtains. Even an hour before falling, there is the chance for that fruit to become more ripe and sweet but the moment it falls every possibility of development comes to an end for it.

The human being is the fruit of nature with all the potentials for that person to be good or bad. If we adopt worship and devotion, we are being ripened. If we sin, we are plagued like a rotten fruit. Repentance is one of the ways by which one is nourished when one is alive, not in death or after it. All the changes and revolution and ups and downs are connected with this world while in the next world, they all come to an end and stop.

Another example is a baby in the mother's womb. All its nourishment and health are through the mother but the moment it is born, total dependence comes to an end and, a new order is established for its life that is quite different from the previous one. In the next world, too, everything is different from the order of this world.

Imām ʻAlī (A.S.)says, 'Today is the time of deeds and not reckoning and tomorrow (in the hereafter) is the time for reckoning and not for deeds.'[1] He does not mean that there is no punishment in this world. Some of the misfortunes which befall us are punishments. But again it does not mean that all punishments for wicked deeds are inflicted in this world.

1. Imām ʻAlī, *Nahj al-Balāghah*, 84.

Therefore, if one receives no punishment here it does not mean that one is quite chaste and that one's account is clear.

On the other hand, if a happening like a flood destroys people, is it due to their deeds and their punishment in the world? No. The above saying of Imām 'Alī (A.S) says that as this world is for deeds and not for reckoning, the next world is for reckoning and not deeds. That is the reason why repentance must take place before death to be valid, that is, it must take place where there is still time and opportunity for it.
God says in the Qur'an,

> He promises them and fills them with fancies but there is nothing Satan promises then? Except delusion. (4: 120)

Repentance from Imām 'Alī's Viewpoint

A man came to Imām 'Alī (A.S) to repent and when the Imām realized that the man was ignorant of the importance of repentance, he said to him, "Do you know the meaning of repentance? It has an exalted position. It has six conditions for its acceptance and the last two are the conditions of its completion." What are those six points?[1]

The first one is regretting what has passed. It means looking at the dark deed and being so sorry and ashamed of it that it makes your heart burn. The Qur'an says:

> Oh believers, wine and arrow-shuffling, idols and divining arrows are an abomination, some of satan's work, so avoid it; haply you will prosper. (5:90)

1. Ibid, 549.

Everyone knows how despicable dead flesh is and there is nothing more fitting than comparing backbiting with it. Calumny is in the same category of sins. Some people in accusing others begin their words by the phrase, "It is said," and suppose that in this way they acquit themselves of the sin of calumny and later on they disclaim their remark and say that they have quoted others' words. This too is a sin and the Qur'an has forbidden it in the following verse.

> Those who love that indecency should be spread abroad concerning those who believe there awaits them a painful chastisement. (24:19)

Those who spread accusations of others are committing a great sin. The same applies to unclean glances at people's wives or daughters to the abandonment of prayer and fasting and showing indifference to sacred rites in the months of mourning and fasting. Being inadequately dressed in public is another such sin.

The Prophet (S) in speaking of his ascension says, "*I saw women there hung by their hair and beaten with fiery scourges and women who were hung by their breasts and beaten with whips.* I asked who they were and was told, 'These are the women who exhibited their bodies in public' ".

Of what worth is this brief span of life to expose oneself to such heavenly punishments. Is it not time to come to oneself, to feel humble and show interest in what is ordained by God? The Qur'an says:

> Is it not time that the hearts of those who believe should be humbled to the remembrance of God and the Truth which He has sent down. (57: 16)

The First Pillar of Repentance: Regret

What is the use of shedding one tear drop occasionally for appearance's sake instead of repenting and checking ourselves and others from sinning?

The First Pillar of Repentance: Decisive Resolution not to Return

The second condition that forms the basis of reference is a decisive resolution not to repeat the foul deed again. Repentance does not depend on the enormity of sin. Every kind of sin, whether big or small, lends itself to repentance provided the Penitent is serious in his or her intention .

The First Condition of Repentance: Returning What Belongs to Others

One of the two conditions for the acceptance of repentance is to return what belongs to others, whether it is something that is seized or a right that has been trampled on. It must either be returned itself or, at least, the rightful owner must be given satisfaction. God will not forget him and the same applies to a person who has been backbitten. He must be given satisfaction. He must accept the apology.

I wish to narrate something that concerns myself. I was a young religious student attending a group in which someone started to slander the late Āyatullāh Ḥujjat whose pupil I had been for years. I felt this to be quite wrong but I did nothing about it. One day I went to his house and asked to see him. I was let in and I explained that he had spoken about him behind his back a great deal and had done nothing to stop them. I felt penitent about it and asked for his forgiveness. With the greatness that this man had, he said, "There are two kinds of slander about people like us, one is an insult to Islam and the other concerns our person." I explained that he had not said anything offensive about Islam but had spoken only of his person. He told me I was forgiven.

In repentance everything that is unlawfully acquired belongs to others whether it is a religious task, bribery or any illegitimate gain or any damage done and it must be repaid and amended so that the rightful owner or the person who has received the damage should be satisfied. If you have nothing left to give back and for example the rightful owner is no longer living, seek forgiveness from God. God willing, He will make that person satisfied.

The Second Condition: Restoring Heavenly Rights

Similarly, heavenly rights must also be restored. What are heavenly rights? If you have failed to observe the fast or perform your ritual prayer or failed to make your obligatory pilgrimage to Mecca in spite of being able to bear it physically and financially, you must make up for all these failures. This is the second condition for the acceptance of your repentance.

A lady who attended one of my discourses had written to me saying that she was deeply influenced by my remarks about a total change of heart. She confessed that in spite of the higher education and her job as the head of a school, she was unfortunate enough not to be properly acquainted with the Qur'an and she asked for guidance and advice.

Allow me to give a general answer. It is necessary for every Muslim to know Arabic in order to understand the Qur'an and his own prayer. But as it happens English is at present the international language and a means of increasing one's income and every school boy and girl is taught that language, while

Arabic is entirely neglected even though it is religiously and spiritually greatly needed by us.

The First Condition of Perfection of Repentance

The next point Imām 'Alī (A.S.) mentioned about the condition for the acceptance of repentance is to rid oneself of all the flesh that has grown on one by illegitimate means. This requires the mortification of the flesh, abstinence and self- discipline. It means benefitting from what is legitimate, honest and proper.

My father narrated that the late Raḍawī Khurasānī, who was a religious sage, had a very corpulent body. In the last years of his life he met a devout ascetic and through his influence, he decided to get rid of his extra flesh to such an extent that he became quite lean and thin. I am not so insolent as to say that his fatness was due to loose living, but anyhow he himself had come to the conclusion that a religious person must not be so corpulent.

The Second Condition of Perfection of Repentance

The last condition that I wish to explain is to let the body which has tasted the sweetness of sin, also taste the pain of deviation and worship. Fasting is not an easy matter especially if you spend the night in prayer.

Two Qur'anic Points

The Qur'an in speaking of repentance mentions the following points:

> God loves those who repent and He loves those who cleanse themselves. (2:222)

This means that you must cleanse yourself not only physically but also spiritually. The Prophet (S) was a fine example of both kinds of cleanliness.

The Qur'an also speaks of reforming oneself in connection with repentance.

> And he who repents, after his evil doing and makes amends, God is All- compassionate. (5:39)

I have already mentioned that sometimes one half of a person rebels against the other half and this rebellion may be by the lower side of a person such as his lust, anger or devilry or by his higher side like his intellect, conscience, his true nature and his depth of heart.

Those who have suffered sexual deprivations in the name of worship and virtue suddenly turn into libertines and make rebels of themselves. But a revolution which is started by a belief in God by recognizing the higher side of the human being, is holy and accompanied by reform.

A Peculiarity of Prophets and Saints

One of the peculiarities of the Prophets as compared with other human leaders is that their revolution is different from a revolution begun by leaders in a society. The latter manage only to arouse one group or class against another class or classes of society and equip them with the means or vanquishing the adversaries. This kind of revolution has its use in cases where a class of oppressors and a class of the oppressed have come into existence. Calling upon the oppressed to seize the right is human and this action has been both recommended and carried out by Islam and all the Prophets. One of the testaments of Imām 'Alī (A.S.)to his two sons, was, "Always be an enemy of an oppressor and an ally of the oppressed."[1]

---

1. Ibid, 421.

But what revolutionary leaders are unable to do what Prophets can do is to arouse the human being against the self and make him or her repent, they can also make the oppressors rise against their own wicked deeds. You meet many figures like Abū Sufyān and Abū Jahl in the history of Islam against whom the poor and weak people have arisen and also tyrants like these have rebelled against themselves.

Bishr Ḥāfī's Repentance

Imām Mūsā Ibn Ja'far was passing through a market in Baghdad. He heard the sound of music and merry-making from a house. As he was passing by it, he saw a girl servant coming out with a bucket of rubbish. He asked her whether the owner of the house was a free man or a slave. The girl was surprised at this question and answered that he was naturally a free man and a man of consequence in that town. It took her some time before she returned to the house. The master asked her why she had been away so long. She told him about her talk with the man and gave a description of him. She said that his last remark was that if the master of the house did not consider himself a free man, he would not engage in such revelry and merry- making.

The man realized by her description that the man was none but the Imām. He gave himself no time even to put on his shoes and hurried to the door, bare-footed to see the Imām. He ran in the direction that he was told the Imām had taken and on catching up with him, knelt down and said, "You were quite right. I am a slave but I knew it not. I want from this hour to be God's slave and begin again with my repentance."

He returned home and threw away all the means of revelry and from then on he walked the streets of Baghdad in his bare feet receiving the nickname, 'the barefooted Bashar'. He was asked the reason for not wearing shoes and he answered, "As I had the honor of meeting the Imām as I am now I wish to preserve the memory of it by going bare-footed."

Abū Lubāba's Repentance

Concerning the affair of the Jewish tribe of the Banī Quraiḍah who had acted treacherously against Islam and the Muslims, the Prophet (S) decided to settle the question for good. They asked him to dispatch Abū Lubābah who had an inclination towards them for consultation. The Prophet (S) agreed and sent him to them. He betrayed this trust by some remark which was in favor of the Jews and against the Muslims. As he was returning to Medina he felt ashamed of his action and went home, not to see his wife and children, but to get a piece of rope to go to the mosque of the Prophet. He tied himself to a pillar and cried, "Oh God I will not untie myself until my repentance is accepted." Only at the time of ritual prayers or to ease nature did his daughter untie him tor a few moments and gave him some food and again he asked to be bound, spending long hours lamenting and regretting what he had done and wishing to be dead unless he was absolved from his sin.

They reported this to the Prophet (S) and he said, "*If he had come to me I would have begged God to forgive him but as he has made a direct request of God, He will deal with him.*" After two or three days, divine revelation informed the Prophet (S) that Abū Lubābah was forgiven. When the people of Medina heard this, they poured into the mosque to release him but he requested the Prophet (S) to do so, which he did.

Those who have made a pilgrimage to Medina know that on one of the pillars of the Prophet's mosque it is written, 'pillar of repentance'. This is the pillar where Abū Lubābah repented and in his time it was a wooden column. After his absolution, Abū Lubābah, as a sign of gratitude offered all his wealth to be used in the way of God but the Prophet (S) did not agree. He offered two-thirds of it. Again the Prophet (S) refused. For the third time he offered one third and the Prophet (S) agreed. This was just since Abū Lubābah had the duty of supporting his family.[1]

It is narrated that a man died and the Prophet (S) went to perform his burial prayer. He asked how many children the man had and what wealth he had left. They said he was well-off but had given away his wealth for charity before his death. The Prophet (S) said, *"If I had known this before, I would not have prayed for him since he has bequeathed hungry children to society."*

It is also said that if a sick man intends to leave more than one third of his wealth to charity, his bequest is not acceptable since he has done so on his death bed even if this is not done by bequest but as an ordinary act of transfer.

I have discussed the question of repentance throughout these nights because these sacred nights of staying awake are the best time for penitence and begging God's forgiveness so that you may be absolved from your sins. But in this repentance all the conditions that I mentioned before must be fulfilled.

Zuhayr Ibn al-Qayn's Repentance

Another example of repentance was Zuhayr Ibn Qayn who became a companion of Imām Ḥusain (A.S.). He was one of the followers of 'Uthmān who believed that Imām 'Alī (A.S.)God

---

1. Muḥammad Bāqir Majlisī, *Biḥār al-Anwār*, vol. 22, 93-4.

forbid, had a hand in the murder of ‘Uthmān. He was returning from Mecca to Iraq and as Imām Ḥusain (A.S.)was taking the same route, he wondered whether he should meet the Imām or not. As he was at heart a true believer he feared that the Imām, as the grandson of the Prophet, might ask him something which he would be unwilling to perform which would be very bad so he kept away from the Imām. But in one of the stopping places on their way they happened to alight by a well at the same time. The Imām sent someone to bring Zuhayr to him. Zuhayr, as the head of the tribe, was dining in his tent with his family and companions. He went pale on hearing the summons and said, "What I did not wish for has happened."

He did not know what to say. He had a wife full of belief who said to him, “Are you not ashamed by showing hesitation in obeying the call of the Prophet's grandson which you should consider an honor? Go at once.” Zuhayr unwillingly arose and went to meet the Imām. No one knows what passed between them but when Zuhayr returned he looked quite a different man. He was now very cheerful and happy. We do not know how the Imām transformed him but a holy revolution had taken place in him. At once he started giving instructions about his will concerning his wealth and members of his family and hastened to join the Imām. In Karbalā he was in the front line of the Imām 's followers, where he achieved martyrdom with them all. When his wife sent a servant with a shroud for his body, the servant saw a shameful sight. They discovered that not only Zubair's body but also his master's body lacked a shroud .

In conclusion I pray to God for a good end for us all and for the chance of true repentance by us and forgiveness by Him.

Discourse 10
Migration and *Jihād* I

> And whoso goes forth from his house as an emigrant to God and His Messenger and then death overtakes him, his wage shall have fallen on God. Surely God is All-forgiving All-compassionate. (4:100)

The holy religion of Islam is based on the two pillars of migration and *jihād* (spiritual and religious struggle upon the way of God). The Qur'an sanctifies both matters and praises profoundly those who migrate.

Migration means leaving one's home and dwelling and Setting off for another destination in order to save religion and faith .This matter is referred to in many verses of the Qur'an. The Muslims of early Islam consisted of two groups: The Emigrants and the Companions. The Companions were

In Medina and the Emigrants were those who left their town and Went to Medina. Migration and *jihād* cannot be abrogated; both are permanent decrees which conditions might at any time make necessary.

Migrating Sins

To remove misunderstanding, let me explain that other

interpretations are also made of both migration and *jihād.* It has been said, " An emigrant is one who abandons sins."[1] Is this meaning proper? If so, then all penitents in the world who avoid sin are emigrants. Two examples may be given here: Fuḍayl Ibn 'Ayāḍ and Bishr Ḥāfī. Fuḍayl was a thief at the beginning but a change of heart made him reject all sins and repent sincerely. Later he was known not only as a virtuous man but as a guide and teacher of others. In his former days he climbed a wall to enter a house where as it happened a devout man kept awake praying and reading the Qur'an. He heard the melodious voice of the man reading a verse of the Holy Qur'an.

When he heard it, sitting on the wall, he thought, "It is a revelation addressed directly to me. Yes, oh God, it is time, this very moment." He climbed down and from that moment on, he abandoned theft, drinking and gambling and whatever other vices he had. He restored as much property as was possible and whatever other vices he had. He restored as much property as was possible to their owners and made up for all his missed acts of worship. Thus, he was an emigrant from sin.

In the time of Imām Mūsā al-Kāẓim(A.S.)there was a man in Baghdad called Bishr Ḥāfī who was a pleasure-loving aristocrat. One day the Imām was passing by this man's house when a maid came out to leave the rubbish somewhere.

At the same time, the sound of music was heard from the house. It seemed that some kind of revelry was going on there. The Imām tauntingly asked whose house it was and whether or not the owner was a slave or a free man. The maid answered in surprise, "Don't you know? This is the house of Bishr Ḥāfī. How could he be a slave?" The Imām said, "He must be free to

1. Muḥammad Ibn Ya'qūb Kulaynī, *Uṣūl min al-Kāfī,* vol. 2, 235.

be engaged thus. If he were a slave his conduct would be different." Then the Imām went on his way.

When the maid returned to the house, Bishr asked why she had been gone so long. She related the conversation she had with a man who, according to her, looked very virtuous and religious. By her description, Bishr realized that it could not have been anyone but the Imām. He felt a sudden change of heart and eagerly asked which direction he had taken. On being told, he ran out bare-footed and managed to catch up with the Imām. He fell at the Imām's feet, sobbing and admitted his interest in being a slave from that minute onward, a slave of God. He repented his past conduct and on returning home, threw away all the implements of revelry and began a life of virtue and devotion. Thus he may be considered another emigrant from sin.

Fighting against Carnal Soul

There is a similar interpretation about *jihād*. It is said that a *mujāhid* (one who engages in religious and spiritual struggle in the way of God) is one who combats the self and fights against his or her carnal desires.

'Alī (A.S.) says, "The bravest person is he who conquers his own desires." One day the Holy Prophet was passing through a street in Medina. He saw a number of youths who were engaged in a contents of lifting a heavy stone. The Prophet (S) asked if they would like him to act as a judge of the contest. They eagerly agreed. Then the Prophet (S) said, "There is no need to lift the stone to see which of you is the strongest. I can say that the strongest person is he who in his desire for a sin is able to control that desire. Such a person is truly a brave warrior."

A story is related about Pūriyā-ye Walī who is considered a great world champion as well as a symbol of chivalry and manliness. Once he had visited another country for a wrestling contest with its champion. In the street he came across an old woman who was offering people sweets as charity and begging them to pray for her son. She approached Pūriyā-ye Walī and offered her sweets. He asked what it was for. She said, "My son is a wrestling champion who is challenged by a champion from another country. We live on the income he gets from wrestling and if he loses this contest, we will have nothing to live on." He said he was at a cross-road whether to show his strength or his manliness in the next day's contest. Although he was far stronger than his adversary, he wrestled in such a way as to let him win. He says that at that moment he suddenly felt that his heart was opened by God and it seemed as if he was surrounded by angels. He fought his own desire and thus joined the rank of saints.

There is another story about ʻAlī (A.S.) and ʻAmar Ibn ʻAbd Wadd, a champion who had stood alone against a thousand men. In the Battle of the Trench, the Muslims were on one side of the trench and the enemy, on the other, so that the enemy could not cross it. A few of the infidels including Amr managed to get to the other side challenging the Muslims who were afraid to face him since they were aware of his strength. The Prophet (S) asked who would take the challenge but no one moved except a young man of 23 or 24 and that was ʻAlī (A.S.). The Prophet (S) did not give him leave.

ʻUmar said to the Prophet (S) that as no one came forth, ʻAlī (A.S.) should be allowed to proceed. ʻAlī (A.S.) faced ʻUmar and knocked this great champion down and sat on his chest to kill him. But ʻUmar spat in ʻAlī's face in anger for his defeat. ʻAlī (A.S.) was offended greatly at this mean conduct. He arose from the enemy's chest and walked about for a while to curb his anger. When ‘Umar asked him the reason for his hesitation, he answered, "I did not wish to kill you in anger for I am fighting for God and in this task there is no room for wrath." This is what a brave warrior is like.

Wrong Interpretation

Another interpretation of the *jihād* is combatting one's self. The Prophet (S) called it the greater *jihād*. But some people were diverted by this interpretation, supposing that migration was only abandoning sin and *jihād* was only against the self. Thus, they forgot that migration also means abandoning an undesirable place and *jihād* also includes fighting foreign enemies. Thus, Islam believes in two kinds of migration and two kinds of *jihād*. If we negate one type of either under the pretext of the other, we are diverted from the teachings of Islam.

The saints of our religion including the holy Prophets, Imām ‘Alī and all the other Imāms were all strivers and migrants. From a spiritual point of view, there are stages which cannot be passed except through these actions. A man who has never entered the field of *jihād* cannot be called a *mujāhid* and one who has not migrated may not win the epithet of an emigrant.

From the view of Islam, marriage is sacred in several practical ways (unlike Christianity where celibacy is considered to be sacred). What is the reason for this? One of the reasons is in educating man's spirit. It is a kind of maturity and perfection which is not obtainable except through marriage. If a man or a woman remains single to the end of his/her life, even if that life is spent in asceticism, devotion, prayer and in combat with vices, there is still a kind of immaturity noticeable in each of them. That is why marriage is recommended as a necessary tradition.

The factors which are efficacious in man's education are so in their proper spheres and none of them can take the place of another. Migration and *jihād*, too, are factors which cannot be replaced by any other factor. Nor can one kind of each factor take the place of the other kind.

Decisive Intention of Migration and *Jihād*

What is the duty of individuals under different conditions? For not all conditions are those of *jihād* and migration.

The Holy Prophet has seen to this and told us that the duty of a Muslim is to be serious in his intention to migrate or enter *jihād* whenever conditions so necessitate it. Thus a person who has never fought or never thought of fighting will in his death pass away in a kind of hypocrisy while those who cherish the intention to migrate or fight in a *jihād* under necessary conditions, may attain the rank of emigrants and crusaders.

The Holy Qur'an says,

> Such believers as sit at home, unless they have an injury, are not the equals of those who struggle in the path of God with their possessions and their selves over the ones who sit at home, yet to each God has promised the reward most fair and God has preferred those who struggle over the ones who sit at home for the bounty of a mighty wage ... (4:95)

What God is telling us here is that the Muslims who are *mujāhids*, fighters in the path of God with their wealth and their lives and those who sit in their homes (in disobedience to the Qur'an) merely on the pretext of 'those who are ready to fight are enough," are not all equal. The Holy Qur'an does not reproach those who sit in their homes due to some excess like blindness or being lame or ill, whose mentalities and intentions are such that if they were not handicapped in this way, they would be the first to rush to *jihād* in the path of God. Perhaps they too have the level of *mujāhids.*

When ‘Alī (A.S.) returned from the Battle of Ṣiffīn, someone came to him and said, "I wish my brother was with you in the battle." ‘Alī said, "What was his intention? Did he have an excuse or not? If he had no excuse for not joining us, all the better that he did not come. But if his heart was with us though he could not join us for a reason, he may be considered to have been with us. “The man said, "He did intend to join you." ‘Alī (A.S.) said, "Then not only was your brother with us but even those who are still in the wombs of their mothers or in the loins of their fathers may be considered as having joined us."

What is meant by 'waiting for the advent?' Some people suppose it to mean waiting for the twelfth Imām to reappear one day with his three hundred and thirteen special companions and other followers to destroy the enemies of Islam, to establish peace and prosperity and perfect freedom, for us to enjoy. What is really meant by waiting for relief (through the advent of the Imām Mahdī) is the hope of joining Imām Mahdī on his reappearance in the holy war and perhaps even attaining martyrdom. That is the hearty wish of every true Muslim and striver. It never means sitting by until everything is put into order and then benefitting from the subsequent blessings. The Prophet's companions said, "We are not like Moses' tribe." When this tribe reached near Palestine, they said to Moses, 'You and your God can go and fight the enemy, and we will sit here until everything is all right." Moses asked, "What do you think is your duty? Your duty is to drive out the enemy who has occupied your home." The Prophet's companions said, "We are not like Moses' tribe. We will do whatever you command." Thus, waiting for relief means aiding Imām Mahdī in fighting and reforming the world.

Many of us in praying wish to have accompanied Imām Ḥusain(A.S.)to have won salvation. Is this claim made in all sincerity? In some cases it is, but in others it is not.

A Dream of a Great Scholar

On the night before his martyrdom, Imām Ḥusain (A.S.)said, "I know of no better and more loyal companions than mine." A great *Shī'ite* man of learning stated that he did not believe the above statement was really made by Imām Ḥusain (A.S.)for, according to them, the Imām 's companions did not do much against the enemy's cruelty. It was the duty of every ordinary Muslim to offer his service to the grandson of the Prophet (S) and 'Alī's son. Those who abstained from assisting him must have been wicked people. This learned man says that God made him realize his mistake by means of a dream. He dreamed that he was in the battlefield of Karbalā and had come to the Imām to offer his services. The Imām told him that he would give him instructions in its proper time. It was the time of the ritual prayer and the Imām told him to stand guard in case the enemy started shooting while the Imāms and his companions performed the noon ritual prayer. Suddenly an arrow was shot towards him and as he bent himself to avoid it, it struck the Imām. He says that in his dream he felt ashamed and penitent in evading the arrow and said he would not do so another time. But he repeated his former action to avoid the next three shots which again struck the Imām 's body. "I never found better and more loyal companions than mine."[1] His companions were men

1. Muḥammad Bāqir Majlisī, *Biḥār al-Anwār*, vol. 44, 392.

of action, not words. On the 10th of Muḥarram, most of Imām Ḥusain's companions had been killed while a few of them and members of his household were still alive by noon.

In the first phase of the battle, the two sides faced each other. The Imām 's side consisted of only 72 warriors but looking valiant and steadfast. The Imām arranged his little army by placing Zuhayr Ibn Qayn at the head of the right flank, Habib on the left flank and his brave brother Abūlfaḍl as his own standard bearer. The commanders asked permission to begin the fight.

Meanwhile 'Umar Sa'd as a commander of the enemy's side had been hesitant about beginning the battle, intending to satisfy both sides. He kept on writing letters to the Imām proposing some kind of compromise. Ibn Ziyād as the enemy's commander-in-chief was annoyed at this conduct and orded him either to act at once or yield the command to someone else.

'Umar Ibn Sa'd fearing that his former procrastination may have caused him loss of face with his superiors as well as the chance of being given the governorship of Rey, tried to make up for it by showing excessive cruelty and was the first man to shoot at the Imām 's tent, calling the men around him to witness this act and report it in his favor to ibn Ziyād.

The late Shaykh Āyatī used to say in his sermons that the Battle of Karbalā began with one arrow, shot by 'Umar Ibn Sa'd and ended with another, when a poisoned arrow struck the Imām on the chest so that he ceased to proclaim his challenge against the enemy and only had time to pray to God. "In the Name of God, in God and for the sake of the nation of the Prophet (S)of God."

One of Imām Ḥusain's companions called 'Ābis Ibn Abī Shabīb

faced the enemy bravely and challenged them. No one dared to take up the challenge. In anger he returned to the camp, took off his battle dress and came back to the battlefield again almost naked and challenged the enemy. Again no one came forth but they treacherously threw stones and broken swords at him and finally killed him.

The Imām's companions showed amazing manliness and loyalty on the last day of the battle. Both men and women created scenes which are unrivalled in human history. 'Abdullāh Ibn 'Umar al-Kalbī was one of these valiant men who had brought his wife and mother with him. When he wanted to set off for the field, his newly wed wife stopped him demanding what would happen to her if he was killed. His mother interrupted her telling him not to pay attention to his wife since that day was a day of trial and if he did not sacrifice himself for the Imāms she would not forgive him as a mother. 'Abdullāh joined the battle and was killed. Then his mother picked up a tent pole and rushed upon the enemy. The Imām told her to return as women were not obliged to fight in Islam and she picked up the head, kissed it and pressed it tightly to her breast, saying, "Well done, my son. I am satisfied with you." Then she threw the head back at the enemy saying, "We do not take back what we have offered in the way of God."

Among those who offered their service to him was a boy of twelve who had tied a sword to his waist asking for leave to fight as his father had already been killed. The Imām said, "I fear that your mother may not be willing." he answered, "It was my mother who gave me leave and told me that if I did not offer my life for the sake of the Imām , she would not forgive me." It was customary for the Arabs to introduce themselves on entering the battlefield but this boy did not do so and remained unknown. His battle cry in the face of the enemy was original for he said, "I am one whose master is Ḥusain and what a good master he is, oh people." He considered this enough. In conclusion I pray to God to illuminate our hearts with the light of faith and make us true migrants and warriors in the religion of Islam and give us victory over its enemies and enable us to win His satisfaction.

Discourse 11
Migration and *Jihād* II

> Whoso goes forth from his house are migrants to God and His Messenger and then death overtakes him, and his wage shall have fallen on God; surely God is All-forgiving, All compassionate. (4:201)

My previous discourse showed that the questions of migration and holy war are frequently mentioned in the Qur'an together. Today I wish to add to my previous remarks concerning the value of these two injunctions in training and perfecting man's spirit ethically and socially. If we wish to discover the spirit of migration and *jihād*, we should remember that migration means freeing oneself from certain attachments which prove themselves to be undesirable and *jihād* means combatting an enemy and the self. Without these two assets, man would be abject and enslaved for living in a basement in a material and spiritual environment shows total lack of spiritual freedom.

Islam Praises Travelling

If we consider migration to mean travelling to other places the question arises whether travelling is better than staying in one place. In Islam, travel is praised though not as a permanent activity similar to a gypsy life. In the same way, staying permanently in a village or a town all one's life is a form of enslavement which is not recommended since it weakens one's soul and spirit. Travel, especially if one is equipped with knowledge gamed at home, is most profitable, while for an ignorant person, it is of little value. Even studying books cannot supply the maturity that travel produces in one's spirit. Without travelling to Islamic countries, for example, we cannot truly know the Islamic world and its problems. Solely through reading is to some extent valuable. Thus the Holy Qur'an tells us, 'Travel in the earth.' (6:11)

Historians are unanimous about the need for the study of history but the Qur'an does not confine the study of history to reading books on history. It recommends visits to historical monuments and relics which are made possible by travel.

In a poem attributed to the first Imām, we are told to travel in the sea of attainment and eminence and that these are five benefits to be had from journeys.[1] These are as follows:

The removal of sorrow from the heart. As long as one sticks to an environment, his mind is full of grief and sadness and for a time at least he feels relieved of their burden.

Earning a livelihood. If you are intelligent enough you can gain a living in travel and improve your financial condition beyond what is possible by staying always in one place.

Earning knowledge. You can also increase your knowledge by travel, by contact with the learned men of the places you visit, by becoming acquainted with their world and thoughts.

---

1. Ḥusain Nūrī al-Tabrisī, *Mustadrak al-Wasā'il wa Mustanbaṭ al-Masā'il*, vol. 8,115.

Earning experience in manners and customs. Travel makes you familiar with all sorts of customs which may seem to you better than your local customs, thereby improving your conduct by selecting ways which seem desirable and appropriate to you.

Earning experience in companionship. There is a special delight of conversation and companionship that is often afforded by travel. This contact with lofty minds may ennoble your spirit.

Thus the phrase in the first line of the poem means "Seeking accomplishments and distinction by leaving one's domicile for travel."

Superiority of Travelers

History shows that men of learning on returning from their travels have gained a polish and maturity which they did not have before. Shaykh Bahā'ī is a good example of versatility among learned men because of his extensive travels. The poet Sa'dī is another traveler who shows his wide knowledge and experience in his works. He spent thirty years of his ninety years of life in studying and another thirty in travel to various parts of the world after which his finest books were produced. In his books *Gulistān* and *Būstān* he made many references to places in India, Arabia and many other countries he had visited and wrote delightful anecdotes about various incidents he had met with here and there.

Rūmī is another much travelled poet who became familiar with various countries and their languages and cultures. But Ḥāfiẓ, in spite of his deeply spiritual poems, shows more limitation of experience since he disliked travel and preferred to spend his life in his beloved Shīrāz. Once he was invited by a ruler of India to visit his country. He went as far as the Persian Gulf and, reconsidering it, decided to return to Shīrāz and stay there.

Obviously there is a difference between Shaykh Bahā'ī who had travelled all over the world and a clergyman who has stayed in Najaf for fifty years. Many of our learned clergymen who have experienced the joys of travel and have come into contact with great religious masters have proved more broad-minded than others whose genius has not been less than theirs but have always lived in limited surroundings.

So, in interpreting migration as abandoning undesirable spiritual conditions, it should not be supposed that this negates the actual abandonment of a place. Both kinds of emigration are important: Freeing oneself geographically from a town, zone, a climate, etc. and freeing oneself from habits and qualities which cause one's enslavement.

Migrating Habits

It is natural for a person to acquire certain habits or follow certain social traditions. Those who smoke usually tell the physician who advises them not to do so that they cannot leave the habit. But this is not manly. One should be able to separate oneself from what is harmful. One is not human if one lacks the ability to migrate from vice.

The late Āyatullāh Ḥujjat was almost a chain smoker and in his waking hours he rarely stopped smoking. He fell ill and the doctors advised him to give up smoking. He said jokingly that he wanted his chest for the sake of smoking and without it had had no need for a chest. They warned him of the danger. He agreed at once to give it up and with one word he changed himself into a migrant from where he had been.

It is related about the Caliph Ma'mūn that he was in the habit of eating soil. The physicians gathered to find a way of curing him from this strange habit. They prepared some kind of concoction and prescribed this and that, but it was of no use. One day a man dressed in patched garments came to their door and said, "I have the remedy for it. A kingly resolution." Ma'mūn felt humiliated and said that it was true and thus got rid of the habit.

Being enslaved by habits and customs is unfortunately more prevalent among women than men such as the ceremonies connected with funerals, weddings, etc. If you ask them why they follow these customs, they say it is a tradition. The meaning of migration is the revival of the human personality and combatting a factor which is the main cause of human abjection. A human being should have enough self-respect not to exchange one's freedom and independence for slavery to an environment or to habits and vices. Thus, migration is a necessary factor of self-refinement.

Struggling and Removing Obstacles

Jihād means struggling, combatting ones desires and removing obstacles. The Qur'an says that when the angels come to take the souls of human beings and see their black records, they ask the reason and human beings answer that they were helpless and lived in a corrupt environment where they could do nothing. The angels answer that this is no excuse. A tree might offer such an excuse because it is stationary and cannot move elsewhere to escape from undesirable surroundings. Even animals cannot offer such an excuse for they are able to migrate. Pigeons, geese, swallows and other birds and animals and even fish keep on moving from one region or climate to another in different seasons. Locusts and other insects, too, migrate in a body to new lands. No living creature ties itself down to the soil and rocks. Why then should a human being do so? It is no excuse to say that the enemy leaves no alternative but subjection and abasement. It is a human being's duty to migrate to a position of strength and then give the enemy the same treatment. This is called *jihād.*

The spiritual interpretation of *jihād* is similar. You advise people not to tell lies and they say it is impossible not to do so. Or you tell them to concentrate on God and holy matters in prayer and not allow themselves to be diverted by other thoughts. Again they think it impossible. Why should a man bear defeat? God has not made him to be vanquished by other creatures. He has given him enough freedom to liberate the self from all kinds of fetters, to fight against one's whims and fancies, against love of pleasure and luxury. The choice is between freedom and subjugation. If you cannot dominate desires and place them under your control, they will dominate you.

What was the philosophy of Imām 'Alī as to asceticism and his renunciation of the world? Just as he had no wish to be vanquished by renowned champions in the field of battle, so he had no desire at all to be in the clutches of desires.

It is related that one day he was passing by a butcher who invited the Imām (A.S.) to take away some fresh meat. The Imām (A.S.) said that he had no money with him. The butcher said, "I can wait for it." 'Alī (A.S.) answered, "And I will tell my stomach to wait." He could easily provide himself with the best food and the finest clothes but he refused to become the slave of worldly things.[1] His wish was to be free from undesirable fetters.

---

1. Imām 'Alī, *Nahj al-Balāghah*, 419.

Today is the day after the anniversary of the martyrdom of Imām Ḥusain (A.S.) and his companions and relatives. All the vices and evils of which man is capable showed themselves in the battlefield of Karbalā. The angels witnessed all of it but God Almighty told them to see the other aspect of it which showed all the virtues and fine qualities that man can show.

The enemy committed unheard of cruelties such as beheading children in front of their mothers or cutting them to pieces. They killed eight of them in this way. One of them was 'Alī Aṣghar, the son of Imām Ḥusain (A.S.). The Imām was holding him in his arms and kissing him farewell. Another child was Qāsim, the son of Imām Ḥasan (A.S.)who was killed in the presence of his mother. Another youth whose death was witnessed by his mother was Ibn 'Abdullāh, the son of Zainab, the sister of Imām Ḥusain (A.S.). His half-brother, too, was killed on the same day. A remarkable thing which shows the lofty mind of this woman is that neither before nor after the martyrdom of her son did she mention this happening while on the death of her brother's son she rushed out of the tent and cried, "Oh my brother and my brother's son."

Another youth who met his death in that battle was the son of Muslim Ibn 'Aqīl whose mother was Ruqayyah, the daughter of Imām 'Alī(A.S.). She witnessed the death of her son. Another youth who was killed after the Imām was a ten year old boy. As he rushed out of the tent and stood there looking stupefied, the enemy ran to him and cut off his head. Another sad event was the death of Imām Ḥasan's son, Abdullah, a ten year old orphan who had never seen his father and had been brought up by Imām Ḥusain (A.S.). As the Imām was in his last dying moments, this boy rushed out of the tent and Zainab, his aunt, could do nothing to stop him. He shouted, "I will not be separated from my uncle." A man with a drawn sword rushed upon the Imām to deal him a death blow. The boy lifted his arm to shield his uncle but the blow of the sword cut off his arm and he cried, "Oh uncle." The Imām said, "Dear nephew, be patient. You will soon join your father's grandfather."

In conclusion, I pray to God to illuminate our hearts with the light of faith, full them with love for you and Your saints, grant our sick ones a speedy recovery, our dead ones, salvation, accept our efforts in mourning for the Imām, guide Muslims and grant us salvation in this and the next worlds.

Discourse 12
Belief in the Unseen

> Those who believe in the unseen and perform the prayer, and expend of that we have provided them... (2:3)

It is customary for us to call an individual believer a *mu'min* by which is meant that he is a devout person who has faith in that he performs all the obligatory acts of devotion as well as recommended acts. In the same way, another person is said to be without faith. There is no harm in using those words like this but the Qur'an, too, uses the same words meaning: Having belief in religion or lack of belief in religion. So we must begin our discussion by considering beliefs as a matter of heart.

> The Qur'an, speaking of a group of nomadic Arabs who came to the Prophet (S)to say, 'We believe,' says 'You believe not, rather say, 'We surrender,' for belief has not yet entered your hearts.'(49:14)

> Is this a belief in God or His Attributes or in His Prophet and revelation or resurrection? All these are parts of belief but the Qur'an sums all these up, 'That is the Book, wherein is no doubt, a guidance for the God-fearing who believe in the unseen....' (2:1)

The Meaning of Unseen

Unseen means hidden. Hidden from what? In this enclosed area what is behind these walls is hidden from us but if we feel sure of what is happening behind them, it is faith in the unseen? No, tomorrow it is hidden from us but if we can predict what is going to happen tomorrow, is this a faith in the unseen? Again, no. What is the unseen then?

In this world, there are things which could be understood through the senses of sight, hearing, touch, smell and taste. We call things perceptible if our senses enable us to know them. Animals, too, possess these senses which are sometimes stronger than man's . Some animals possess a sharper sight than man. A dog has a very sensitive ear and power of smell. The tiny ant can easily find its way to a piece of meat by its strong power of smell. But these powers are not related to the unseen. Belief in the unseen means admitting that in the world of existence there are certain facts which we cannot distinguish by our senses, even if they are present before us. The senses given to living creatures are only limited means of contact with the world outside each being. The eyes are given to distinguish form, color and direction. The ears are meant to distinguish waves of sound. The other senses, too, are bestowed for various purposes. But if we cannot distinguish other facts beyond the senses, can we say that they do not exist?

No. This is wrong. The greatest mistake made by the human being is to suppose that all the senses that one has are adequate for understanding whatever exists and to negate what is not distinguishable for one. All the things which a human being should believe in are expressed by the Qur'an under the heading of the unseen. If we cannot distinguish them through the senses, how should we accept them? Other ways and means are placed at our disposal to believe in the unseen. The verse of the Qur'an concerning faith in the unseen does not mean that we should accept every hidden matter simply because we have faith. If an exorcist claimed that he had an army of jinn, we should not believe him simply because he speaks of the unseen. But we must not deny the unseen altogether.

The Way of Believing in the Unseen

If we were asked what are the ways of believing in the unseen, we would say that there are stages. The first stage is to distinguish the various signs which make it impossible to deny it. It means entering from the stage of denial into the stage of doubt.

Let me give you an example. In the past, the only wave which was recognized in the space was the sound wave, which was compared to the waves created by throwing a stone into a pool. But today, science has discovered other waves which are not distinguishable by our ears or any of our other senses such as electric waves or radio waves which are not sound waves. For if they were sound waves it would take a space of time similar to sound waves in order to be heard. It is sometimes said that the sound of Big Ben in London is heard all over the world before it is heard by the people in the area near it.

How can one distinguish various waves in the space which are not sound waves? Only by scientific conjecture, not by the senses. Thus the denial of the existence of such waves shows only ignorance.

Is faith in the unseen a belief in God, in the angels, in the Book and revelation, in the Resurrection? No. It is higher than that. It means belief in a relationship between oneself and the unseen and not thinking of the two as totally separate. When in our prayer we say, 'You only do we serve; to You alone do we pray for succour.' (1:5) we show that we worship hidden God and beg His assistance since we believe that all powers are in His hand. In a supplication you ask His aid to give strength to your body, your resolution and your thought. But what is that for?

It is said that the difference between divine philosophy and religion is that the former may at most believe that there is God apart from the universe, while the main thing in religion is the relationship between a creature and its Creator, between us and the unseen that it establishes and which inclines us to action and effort to serve and, at the same time, tells us that because of our relationship with the unseen we are somehow helped through our supplications to attain our goal. It tells us to be charitable, for it removes calamity . It tells us to supplicate. Of course, the prayer requires certain conditions in order to be fulfilled.

Assistance from the Unseen Is Not Groundless

We cannot sit down and beg for assistance from the unseen.

The Qur'an speaking of the Prophet (S)says:

> Remember God's blessing upon you when you were enemies and He brought your hearts together so that by His blessing you became brothers. You were upon the brink of a pit of fire and He delivered you from it ... (3:98-99)

This is assistance from the unseen. Sometimes you feel that if you follow a certain goal appointed by God, you receive some hidden aid and support beyond what you think or understand, and such a belief gives one a footing which is most necessary in life.

A Story from Āyatullāh Burūjirdī

I remember something about Āyatullāh Burūjirdī, a truly virtuous and fine authority to be imitated in religious matters. He was a monotheist of the highest rank and had a deep conviction and trust in God's aid to man. He had vowed that if he was cured after a surgical operation, he would make a pilgrimage to Mashhad. He announced his intention to his companions one day and asked who would accompany him. We discussed it among ourselves and did not think it advisable for him to make this visit since at that time he was not so well-known and we did not think he would receive the welcome he deserved there. We thought this vow could be fulfilled one or two years later when conditions were more favorable.

Another day when he repeated his invitation, one of us told him that as he was recovering from his illness, it was too soon to go on a long journey by car. He understood the real reason why his friends did not advise the journey. He was aroused enough to say that for seventy years God had favored him, not because of his own deliberations but because it was his lot. He said, "I have always thought what my duty is in the way of God. I have never considered whether it is above or below my dignity to act in a certain way. Whatever happens is my destiny. It is unbecoming to plan my steps at the age of seventy when I have God and His Favor. When I look upon myself as His servant, He will not forget me. Yes. I will depart." And we knew that he arose to the highest point of respect and appreciation by all Muslims.

God has never left the world without a master. Whenever mankind is in real danger, He saves them through a human being. You know how pessimistic the enlightened people of the world have become concerning the future of mankind. Do you know that this pessimism is fitting by the standard of apparent causes and factors? We Muslims do not appreciate this blessing so that, like our ancestors of a hundred years ago, we say the world will last another thousand or a hundred thousand years more.

Intellectual's Pessimism about Future of the World

Some enlightened people claim that the downfall of humanity is near and Einstein is one who believes in this. He says that man will in all probability destroy himself with all the skill at his command for western scientific progress has given the power to destroy mankind.

In the past, this power of destruction was very limited. Ḥajjāj Ibn Yūsuf managed to kill 30,000 people. Neron burned Rome but could he burn the whole world? Today, however, a mad dictator could annihilate the whole of humanity. Hitherto in a war, one side has been victorious and the other side, defeated. But in the next world war, there will be no victory and defeat for both sides will be destroyed. These apparent reasons make us agree with the pessimist.

There is, however, an inspiration that we receive from religion. We see that in the past great dangers have occurred on smaller scales proportionate to the size of tribes, countries or regions. But God has always protected mankind and even when a danger appears on a world wide scale, again God is there to save it. Gandhi says that Europe is full of both madness and genius at the same time. Their madmen are geniuses and their geniuses are madmen.

Bright Future from a Religious Perspective

The logic of religion tells us that we should not worry about the future of mankind. God has given us the promise of a time when wisdom will rule and life will be longer and health and security more complete. The earth is so full of hidden resources that it can provide for many times more than four or five billion people.

The world that is promised to us is a wide and clear space beyond the dark tunnel which is our present world. There is no probability of corruption and vice ruling the whole world. The aid of the unseen for a person is on a personal scale; for communities on a social scale and, the world, on a universal scale. A single world government will establish wholesale justice, security, welfare, progress and goodness.

I pray to God to grant us faith to wait for the Imām who is our savior, and faith in the rightfulness of the Prophet's household and make us familiar with the truths of the holy religion of Islam.

Bibliography

The Holy Qur'an.

'Abd al-Wāḥid al-Āmudī, *Ghurar al-Ḥikam wa Durar al-Kalim*, (Qum: Daftar-e Tablīghāt-e Islāmī, 1366 S.A.H.).

Al-Ḥurr al-'Āmilī, *Wasā'il al-Shī'ah*, (Qum: Āl al-Bayt li 'Iḥyā' al-Turāth, 1409 A.H.).

Arthur, Christense, *L'Iran sous les sassanides (Iran dar Zamān Sāsāniyān)*, trans. Rashīd Yāsimī (Tehran: Chāp Rangīn, 1317 S.A.H).

Āyatullāh Nā'īnī, *Tanbīh al-Ummah wa Tanzīh al-Millah* (Qum: Būstān Kitāb, 1388 S.A.H.).

F. al-Ṭurayḥī, *Majma' al-Baḥrayn*, (Tehran: al-Maktaba al-Murtaḍawiyya 1375 S.A.H).

Ḥusain Nūrī al-Tabrisī, *Mustadrak al-Wasā'il wa Mustanbaṭ al-Masā'il*, (Beirut: Mu'assasah Āl al-Bayt li Iḥyā' al-Turāth, 1408 A.H.).

Ibn Abī'l-Ḥadīd, *Sharḥ Nahj al-Balāghah*, (Qum: Maktabah Āyatullāh al-Mar'ashī al-Najafī, 1404 A.H).

Imām 'Alī, *Nahj al-Balāghah*, ed. Ṣ. al-Ṣāliḥ (Qum: Dār al-Hijrah, 1407 A.H.).

Jalāl al-Dīn Muḥammad Mawlawī, *Mathnawī*, ed. Nicholson, (Tehran: Peymān, 1385 S.A.H.), Book V, verses 3571-2.

Muḥammad Bāqir Majlisī, *Biḥār al-Anwār*, (Beirut: Mu'assasah al-Wafā, 1404 A.H.).

Muḥammad Ibn al-Ḥasan Al-Ḥurr al-'Āmilī, *Wasā'il al-Shī'ah ilā Taḥṣīl Masā'il al-Sharī'ah*, (Tehran: Kitāb-furūshi-ye Islāmiyyah, 1403 A.H.).

Muḥammad Ibn Ya'qūb Kulaynī, *Uṣūl min al-Kāfī*, (Tehran: Dār Kutub al-Islāmiyyah, 1365 S.A.H).

Mullā Muḥsin al-Fayḍ al-Kāshānī, *al-Maḥajjat al-Bayḍā' fī Tahdhīb al-Iḥyā'*, (Beirut: Mu'assasat al-A'lamī li'l-Maṭbū'āt, 1403 A.H.).

Sayyid Ibn Ṭāwūs, *Luhūf 'alā Qatlā al-Ṭufūf*, (Tehran: Jahān, 1348 S.A.H.).

Shaykh 'Abbās Qummī, *Mafātīḥ al-Janān*, (Tehran: Peymān Āzādī, 1372 S.A.H).

Shaykh Muṣliḥ al-Dīn Sa'dī, *Gulistān*, (Tehran: Amīr Kabīr, 1365 S.A.H).

Index

A

'Abdullāh Ibn 'Umar al-Kalbī, 124
'Ābis Ibn Abī Shabīb, 124
Abraham, 81
Abū 'Abdullāh, 86
Abū Baṣīr, 71
Abū Dharr, 6, 8
Abū Jahl, 110
Abū Lubābah, 111, 112
Abū Rayḥān al-Bīrūnī, 54
Abū Sufyān, 110
Abul Faḍl al-'Abbās, 98
Abūlfaḍl, 123
Alexander the Great, 55
'Alī, 7, 8, 10, 11, 17, 27, 28, 29, 36, 37, 38, 39, 44, 45, 50, 55, 58, 59, 60, 61, 62, 63, 64, 67, 68, 69, 71, 72, 73, 77, 78, 82, 83, 85, 92, 93, 95, 96, 97, 101, 103, 104, 108, 109, 112, 117, 118, 119, 121, 122, 132, 133
allāhu akbar, 81, 82
America, 18, 35, 49
Amīr al-mu'minīn, 37
'Amar Ibn 'Abd Wadd, 118
'Amr Ibn Ḥarīz, 78
anṣār, 47
Anbār, 62
Anūshīravān, 38
'Āshūrā, 85
Āyatullāh Burūjirdī, 139
Āyatullāh Ḥujjat Kūh Kamarī, 48, 106, 130
Āyatullāh Nā'īnī, 33

B

Banī Quraiḍah, 111
Bishr Ḥāfī, 116
Buddhism, 60
Busr Ibn Arṭāt, 92
Būstān, 129

C

Christensen, 38
Christianity, 7, 60, 80, 119
compassion, 15, 58

D

Ḍirār, 67

E

Europe, 18, 140

F

freedom, 9, 11, 13, 15, 19, 20, 27, 29, 30, 33, 34, 35, 36, 38, 41, 42, 43, 45, 46, 47, 50, 51, 52, 62, 83, 121, 127, 131, 132
Fuḍayl Ibn 'Ayāḍ, 116

G

Gandhi, 140
Gulistān, 43, 129

H

Ḥāfiẓ, 14, 44, 93, 129
Ḥāj Mīrzā 'Alī Āqā Shīrāzī, 93
Ḥajjāj Ibn Yūsuf, 140
Happy Organization, 23
Ḥātam Ṭā'ī, 44
Hiroshima, 49, 92
Historians, 128
Holy Qur'an, 19, 25, 28, 31, 32, 82, 116, 120, 128
Ḥurr Ibn Yazīd Riyāḥī, 98

I

Ibn 'Aāṣ, 33
Ibn Ḥusain, 64
Ibn Sīnā (Avicenna), 54
Ibn Ziyād, 98, 123
Iṣfahān, 48
Imām Mūsā al-Kāẓim, 116
Imām Ṣādiq, 49, 59
Imām Ḥasan, 11, 58
Imām Ḥusain, 53, 65, 85, 112, 122, 123
Imām Ja'far Ṣādiq, 71
Imām Mahdī, 121
Imām Mūsā Ibn Ja'far, 110
Iqbal Lahouri, 60
Ismā'īl, 81

J

jihād, 115, 116, 117, 119, 120, 121, 127, 132
justice, 11, 13, 15, 65, 75, 76, 78, 79, 141

K

Ka'ba, 80
Kant, 11
Karbalā, 23, 86, 97, 98, 113, 122, 123, 133
Kāshān, 48
Khwājah Rabī', 64
Kūfa, 98

L

Lailā, 46

M

Majnūn, 46
Ma'mūn, 131
Manicheanism, 60
man's awareness, 7
Mashhad, 1, 48, 64, 139
Mathnawī, 10, 20, 28
mawlā, 27, 28
Medina, 10, 47, 111, 115, 117
Mīrzā Shīrāzī, 51
Moses, 32, 33, 36, 102, 121
mū'adhdhin, 73
Mu'āwiyah, 6, 8, 58, 62, 65, 67, 92
Muḥarram, 62, 85, 98, 123
mujāhid, 117, 119
Mullā Ḥusain Qulī Hamadānī, 51
Mullā Ṣadrā, 17
Muslim Ibn 'Aqīl, 133

N

Nahj al-Balāghah, 1, 7, 8, 11, 36, 47, 50, 58, 63, 82, 95, 103, 132
Najaf, 48, 130
Neron, 140
Nietzche, 58

P

peace, 15, 16, 36, 53, 82, 86, 99, 121
Pharaoh, 32, 33, 36, 102
philosophy of humanitarianism, 16
the Prophet (S), 10, 47, 63, 64, 69, 70, 85, 86, 94, 111, 112, 117, 118
prophethood, 34
Pūriyā-ye Walī, 118

Q

Qāsim, 133
Qibla, 80
Qum, 1, 2, 3, 93

R

Raḍawī Khurāsānī, 108
Rome, 140
Rūmī(Jalāl al-Dīn Rūmī),10, 28 , 13, 20, 42, 46, 96, 129
Ruqayyah, 133

S

Sa'īd bin 'Abdullāh Ḥanafī, 86
Sabeans, 32
Sa'dī, 13, 43
Sanā'ī, 76
Sāsāniyān, 38
Sayyid Ḥusain Kūh Kamarī, 48
self- purification, 34
self-contemptuous, 59
self-sacrifice, 7

Shaykh Anṣārī, 48
Shaykh Āyatī, 123
Shaykh Bahā'ī, 129, 130
Shi'ite, 122
Shīites, 28
Shimr, 23
Shīrāz, 23
Ṣiffīn, 37, 58, 121
spiritual freedom, 27, 33, 34, 36, 41, 51
spirituality, 15, 21, 37, 38
Sulṭān Maḥmūd, 54
Sunnīs, 28

T

Taḥqīq-e mā lil-Hind, 54
Tanzīh al-ummah, 33

U

'Ubaidullāh Ibn 'Abbās, 92
'Ubidullāh Ibn Ziyād, 98
'Uday Ibn Ḥātam, 67
'Umar Ibn Sa'd, 98, 123
Umayyids, 33
ummah, 33
Umm-e Ḥamīda, 71
Umm-e Salamah, 94
'Uthmān, 112

V

virtue, 14, 34, 36, 109, 117

Y

Yazīd, 23, 65

Z

Zainab, 133
Ziyād, 62, 123
Zubair, 113
Zuhayr Ibn Qayn, 112, 123

www.ingramcontent.com/pod-product-compliance
Lightning Source LLC
Chambersburg PA
CBHW030302100526
44590CB00012B/484
9781922583666